D0587326

early years
training &
management

Planning, assessing and record-keeping

Pauline Kenyon

Editor	Author	Illustrations
Victoria Lee	Pauline Kenyon	Simon Rumble
Assistant Editor	**Series Designer**	**Cover Photography**
Aileen Lalor	Mark Udall	Mark Udall

Designer
Andrea Lewis

Acknowledgement:
Qualifications and Curriculum Authority for the use of extracts from the
QCA/DfES document *Curriculum guidance for the foundation stage*
© 2000 Qualifications and Curriculum Authority; Qualifications and Curriculum
Authority for the use of extracts from the QCA/DfES document *Foundation Stage
Profile* © 2002, Qualifications and Curriculum Authority.

Text © 2004 Pauline Kenyon
© 2004 Scholastic Ltd

Designed using Adobe InDesign

Published by Scholastic Ltd, Villiers House,
Clarendon Avenue, Leamington Spa, Warwickshire CV32 5PR

Visit our website at www.scholastic.co.uk

Printed by Bell & Bain Ltd. Glasgow

1 2 3 4 5 6 7 8 9 0   4 5 6 7 8 9 0 1 2 3

British Library Cataloguing-in-Publication Data A catalogue record for this book is available from the British Library.
ISBN 0 439 97138 1
The right of Pauline Kenyon to be identified as the author of this work has been asserted by her in accordance with the Copyright, Designs and Patents Act 1988.

Contents

Photocopiable pages

early years
training & management

Introduction

About this book

This book has been designed to help early years practitioners, in a wide variety of different settings, in several important areas – planning the best curriculum provision to meet the needs of children from very different backgrounds and of varying abilities (including children with special educational needs), building in methods of productive assessment and developing an effective record-keeping system. There is a strong emphasis on developing the professional skills of all staff and in working in positive partnerships with parents, helpers and other agencies. The management of developing all these aspects is stressed throughout all recommendations.

Firstly, the book aims to help practitioners plan the most appropriate curriculum for their own children and to help them make sense of the requirements that apply to their settings. It links advice closely with the requirements of the *Curriculum Guidance for the Foundation Stage* (QCA) *Planning for Learning in the Foundation Stage* (QCA) as well as meeting OFSTED inspection expectations for early years settings.

Secondly, it tackles how to develop your setting's approach to the increasingly vital areas of assessing children's attainment and progress, linking this in a realistic manner to your planned programmes. Most experienced early years staff already have a wealth of informal assessment experience to call on, and they make judgements every day they work at the setting. However, they can still feel rather uncomfortable about developing a more formalised assessment structure. This book focuses on 'demystifying' the assessment process and making it the useful tool it should be – a way of gleaning information that helps practitioners to plan for the next steps in their children's learning. Once more, guidance is closely linked to the *Curriculum Guidance for the Foundation Stage* and, importantly, this is strongly referenced to the *Foundation Stage Profile Handbook* (QCA) and new assessment requirements. Additionally, practitioners subject to OFSTED inspections will find that all advice is compatible with inspection requirements.

Finally, the book suggests a range of ideas for how you could record information in a manageable and useful way. The advice and guidance given is very practical and is based on strategies that are tried and tested, workable and best practice in effective early years settings. Suggestions are made for how a range of other agencies can be involved and how settings can best pass on their own records. Ideas for developing parental partnerships and sharing assessment and record-keeping are also explored.

Which practitioners can it help?

The guidance covers issues for a broad range of settings, including playgroups, private nursery groups and schools, and nursery and Reception classes in local authorities. It covers the requirements of the *Foundation Stage Profile* in some detail (which all Reception classes must complete by the end of their summer term), but with many practical ideas for implementing the processes. However, it also acts as a 'user-friendly' guide to organising simple, effective assessment systems in those other settings not bound by this statutory requirement – including voluntary groups that meet in shared accommodation. Whatever the nature of your early years setting, you should find chapters and sections to help you enhance your curriculum planning and develop down-to-earth assessment and record systems.

The book could also provide useful ideas for teacher mentors and other early years practitioners who have responsibility for professional development and training, because it offers a range of staff training activities and shares examples of best practice. It should also prove helpful for school early years coordinators and senior staff, who have overseeing responsibility for Foundation Stage classes within their school.

All the chapters have an accompanying range of photocopiable sheets that have been created to help busy practitioners save time and effort. Most of these can be used repeatedly and can form a bank of planning, assessment and record materials for use at different times throughout the year. Some photocopiable sheets are specifically designed for helpers and parents to use, or for settings to compile summaries to pass on to other agencies, for example, when seeking additional support for a child with special educational needs.

Early years requirements and current issues

Early years practitioners from all settings have welcomed the recent increased recognition of the vital importance of their work with young children. Although practitioners and parents have always known that the quality of young children's learning experiences set the seal on their further development, this has been properly highlighted with the establishment of the official Foundation Stage.

This book should give staff and managers very practical guidance which links well with current requirements and the higher public profile of best practice in early years provision, as well as advice on involving all staff, parents and carers.

The *Curriculum Guidance for the Foundation Stage* clearly outlines the six Areas of Learning that should be every young child's entitlement in settings receiving funding, namely: Personal, social and emotional development; Communication, language and literacy; Mathematical development; Knowledge and understanding of the world; Physical development and Creative development. This is supplemented by *Planning for Learning in the Foundation Stage* (QCA), which gives more information about the levels of planning that are expected in early years settings seeking funding.

The status of early years education has now been officially recognised. The *Foundation Stage Profile Handbook* (QCA) makes clear that the Foundation Stage for three- and four-year-olds is now established as a statutory stage of the National Curriculum for England, alongside Key Stages 1–4. Reception classes in schools are now clearly expected to plan their curriculum and learning programmes to meet the specific needs of young children in the Foundation Stage, following the elements of the six Areas of Learning. This finally removes any previous confusion in schools and takes away the pressure to introduce young children to an unsuitable, and often counter-productive, formal curriculum too soon. It also releases Reception staff from the sometimes difficult struggle to draw out workable and appropriate learning programmes based in a 'watered down' Key Stage 1 curriculum! It enables Foundation Stage managers, and early years coordinators, in primary schools to lead the whole school to an understanding of the most appropriate educational provision for their youngest children and how this provides a firm base for all further learning.

How to use this book

The book has been designed to be flexible enough to meet the different needs of practitioners working in a variety of settings. It can also be used to guide settings that are at quite different levels of development in all, or just some, aspects of curriculum planning, assessment and record-keeping. Managers will be able to decide which approach to take with staff. You could select those sections that are particularly pertinent to your setting for in-depth coverage, whilst choosing other, more familiar parts as a checklist to review your current provision.

A setting that is at an early stage in most areas, or has a significant number of new staff, might find working through the book chapter by chapter useful. This could form the basis of an effective staff professional development and training programme. The book has been constructed so that it can be followed from start to finish, guiding practitioners step by step through the different layers of the planning and assessment process. Managers could plan to hold staff-training sessions of around an hour, using one or two sections of a chapter at each one. Alternatively, a chapter, and all related activities, could be covered comfortably during a full day's training.

Settings which feel they have developed well in many areas covered by the book, might feel it more appropriate to dip into specific sections where they think there are remaining issues to address, and the book will also aid this approach. All chapters have cross-referenced text and this will advise practitioners to consider other related pages, sections or photocopiable sheets, where this would be helpful for them. If there are sections that should be read before embarking on any new section, these are also clearly identified, so you should not miss any important information by 'dipping in'! This book has been designed to take the reader from the essential planning process on to assessment, stressing that you need to know what you are going to assess and how this will be done. Assessment should never be tackled in isolation to learning. The skill of assessment is in judging each child's attainment – and then deciding how their learning will be improved by your planning the next steps, activities and experiences you will provide to help them make good progress. In most sections, you will find best practice examples, models or case studies and checklists to help you review your own practice and consider adopting some of the additional ideas suggested in this book.

The photocopiable sheets

The photocopiable sheets are all referred to within the various sections, with advice on how to maximise their use (for example, several sheets can be used for more than one purpose). The sheets can provide settings with a bank of materials to use over time. Some, like the 'Audit your provision' sheets, can be used on an annual basis to check that your provision coverage is good. Others, such as the 'Six Areas of Learning assessment focus sheets', can be used as an ongoing means to record observations and information collection. Many of them, such as the 'Parents' home Activity sheets', can be used in their own right, but may well stimulate staff to produce personalised additional examples.

The pattern of the book

➤ Chapter 1 covers effective curriculum planning. This chapter is concerned with ensuring that settings have the full and required curriculum coverage. There is a strong emphasis on the key requirements of the six Areas of Learning, what this looks like in practice, and how to plan effectively. There is practical guidance to help you check that your current provision is adequate or to adjust any areas which need alteration or development. Advice also focuses on how to tailor your provision to meet the needs of your unique intake, and how to use the resources available to you in your locality to best effect. A section is dedicated to issues and strategies for planning for play and through related themes. An important element concentrates on planning support programmes for those children with identified special educational needs.

➤ Chapter 2 picks up the essential theme of planning for assessment within your curriculum programmes, so that assessment becomes a normal part of your procedures – properly linked to improving children's learning – and not just a 'bolt on' activity. Advice covers the timings of an effective assessment cycle, nursery provision and establishing 'value added' measures. A section is devoted to SEN assessment and curriculum provision. There is also guidance for Reception classes using the *Foundation Stage Profile*, on planning for literacy and numeracy sessions and dealing with OFSTED. Other settings have specific guidance appropriate to their different assessment issues.

➤ Chapter 3 concentrates on setting up manageable assessment systems with very practical guidance and suggestions for carrying out entry assessment. The related photocopiable sheets provide a firm structure for a workable system.

➤ Chapter 4 focuses on making everyday assessment productive, with sensible ideas for targeting groups and individuals, as well as ways to assess those areas of undirected and outdoor play activities that can be more easily missed by busy practitioners. It also looks at how staff can be used most effectively and how settings can beneficially involve children in assessing their own learning.

➤ Chapter 5 takes assessment logically on to record-keeping and recording. This chapter explores different forms of records and how to build them up. It considers what should be recorded and how parents and carers can be involved in the process. The importance of summary records and passing on information is also thoroughly covered.

➤ Chapter 6 looks at the productive ways to involve a range of staff, parents, carers and other colleagues, in assessment. The importance of liaising with special needs support services is highlighted, with suggestions for effective observation records. A section is devoted to helping staff refine observation skills and a further section is designed to improve the quality of home links and parents'/carers' understanding of assessment in helping their children make the best possible progress.

Chapter 1 Effective curriculum planning

> ➤ **Building your curriculum**
> ➤ **The six Areas of Learning – key requirements**
> ➤ **Auditing your current provision**
> ➤ **Matching your curriculum to your children's needs**
> ➤ **Planning for special educational needs (SEN)**
> ➤ **Using vital local resources**
> ➤ **The planning cycle and systems**
> ➤ **Using staff effectively**

Building your curriculum

What is required?

In recent years there has been a much greater emphasis placed on the importance of the provision of a broad and exciting curriculum, relevant to the needs of young children. The *Curriculum Guidance for the Foundation Stage* (QCA) has been welcomed by early years practitioners in a wide variety of settings. It gives a clear outline of the key elements that should be present in any setting's curriculum but, importantly, it does not prescribe an early years curriculum. Your setting needs to establish a curriculum that has been created and personalised to meet the developmental needs and interests of your children, linked to the use of your local environment, available resources and the community you serve.

The *Curriculum Guidance* highlights the six Areas of Learning that should be provided for children under five, namely:

➤ Personal, social and emotional development
➤ Communication, language and literacy
➤ Mathematical development
➤ Knowledge and understanding of the world
➤ Physical development
➤ Creative development.

It is important that all Areas are included in any setting's provision, so that all children enjoy the broad and relevant range of experiences and opportunities needed for a rounded early years education.

Creating a proper balance

If your setting is seeking funding, one of the requirements is that your curriculum is securely founded on the *Curriculum Guidance* and that all six Areas of Learning are properly balanced. This means, for example, that children engage in a good range of creative activities (art, dance, music and role-play), which extend their learning in this Area. It also means that they have carefully planned opportunities for gross and fine motor development in indoor and outdoor physical tasks. The overall balance should ensure that one or two Areas – in Reception classes, often Communication, language and literacy and Mathematical development – receive an appropriately high emphasis without dominating the curriculum to the detriment of the other Areas of Learning.

Early Learning Goals and Stepping Stones

The *Curriculum Guidance for the Foundation Stage* indicates the Early Learning Goals in each Area of Learning, and emphasises the developmental stage most children are expected to reach by the end of their Reception year in school. However, there is an acceptance that some children will have exceeded these goals, whereas others – possibly the youngest, or those who have spent less time in Foundation Stage settings, or children with special educational needs – may still be working towards some, or all of them.

This is why the Stepping Stones, leading to the Early Learning Goals, are colour-coded to highlight the appropriate progression in learning. Broadly speaking, the yellow band is where most three-year-olds are likely to be operating, the blue band normally represents the developmental stage for four-year-olds, and the green band will more generally reflect the attainment of five-year-olds. Each Early Learning Goal is, therefore, the final Stepping Stone for the end of the Foundation Stage. The function of the Stepping Stones is to give practitioners a useful ladder of progression from each stage to the next, building on children's previous learning in a systematic manner. Essentially then, Stepping Stones should be used to ensure that your planned activities give the children in your setting opportunities to experience relevant learning at the appropriate stage and age.

OFSTED inspectors will expect that the Stepping Stones are used in your planning and will look to see how you incorporate these into your programmes for children of different ages and experience. Moreover, the *Foundation Stage Profile* introduced in 2003, which must be completed as a summative assessment of each child's attainment by the end of the Reception-class year, is linked closely to the Stepping Stones. Other settings catering for younger children will need to assess children's progress measured against the different Stepping Stones and pass on this information to the next providers.

The Foundation Stage Profile

This record covers the six Areas of Learning and is based upon statutory assessment scales, which are derived from component parts of the Stepping Stones. Although settings do not have to use the *Foundation Stage Profile* for ongoing assessment, there is a requirement to complete one for each child during the summer term of the Reception year. This *Profile* must form the basis for reports to parents/carers and for information to be passed on to subsequent teachers. Reporting a child's progress to parents or carers is a key requirement and the *Foundation Stage Profile* can be used instead of other forms of written report at the end of the school year. Issues and advice related to the use of the *Foundation Stage Profile* and implications for settings other than Reception classes will be found in greater detail in Chapters 2 and 5 in this book.

Nurseries and mixed-age settings

Each setting is unique and there will be considerable variation in the numbers of children from different age groups within it. In fact, the balance may well alter over time as some children move on to new settings and others join your setting. This means that the curriculum will need to be tailored to your intake. If you cater for both three- and four-year-olds, you will need to consider how this will affect your planning. Many settings plan their curriculum linked to themes that span a two-year period. The programme is planned to encompass the full range of Areas of Learning, to be covered and revisited over time. The older children who have engaged in the earlier work can be expected to achieve at a higher level during the second theme.

The six Areas of Learning – key requirements

Personal, social and emotional development
- Curriculum Guidance for the Foundation Stage -

Success in this area is vital for young children as it underpins their overall learning within the setting and in all aspects of their lives. Young children need the security of knowing how to behave, to take responsibility for their actions, how to relate to others productively and have experiences which help them to grow in confidence. They need to know what is expected of them within a consistent structure and safe environment, where adults provide good role models and children learn how to succeed.

There is no prescribed curriculum laid down, but settings will need to ensure that they build activities and experiences into their programmes that enable children to:

➤ feel safe and secure and to trust those who work with them
➤ learn to respect themselves and others
➤ develop a positive self-image because their own and other cultures are valued
➤ learn how to acquire social skills and relate positively to others
➤ increase their sensitivity to others and learn how to be a good friend
➤ develop a positive disposition to learning which motivates them
➤ have opportunities to make choices and solve problems.

In order to do this, practitioners have a vital responsibility to:

➤ be positive role models to influence young children
➤ adapt tasks to build on children's own interests and meet learning needs
➤ plan activities that are appropriately challenging
➤ have good communication skills, extending children's vocabulary
➤ encourage good manners and social skills
➤ use open-ended questions to help children think deeply
➤ provide engaging role-play opportunities
➤ create a stimulating environment where all children are valued
➤ encourage children's independence and self-confidence.

Many of these elements will be reflected in an effective setting's general approach to its work, but they cannot be left to chance. Use the 'Audit your provision for Personal, social and emotional development' photocopiable sheet on page 97 to check that your general organisation, pattern of the day and activities, themes, resources, internal and external environment and adult interaction arrangements lend themselves to learning in this crucial area.

Communication, language and literacy
Very young children express their feelings and needs firstly through non-verbal communication, relying greatly on body language and gesture. As children develop, they learn to listen and to speak, describing feelings and thoughts more precisely and learning to interact with others. The effective development of communication and language skills lie at the heart of young children's learning, enabling them to make sense of all other areas of their experience and leading to understanding. The Stepping Stones in this Area of Learning indicate the general progression pathway children follow as they become more confident and competent in

Useful tip
This Area of Learning is about emotional well-being, knowing who you are and where you fit in and feeling good about yourself.

Useful tip
Use the 'Audit
your provision for
Communication,
language and literacy'
photocopiable sheet on
page 98.

all types of communication. These offer a clear incremental ladder of skill acquisition and are extremely useful in curriculum planning, particularly for devising and organising focused activities for small target groups of children at certain stages of development. However, practitioners need to provide the curriculum framework to support the learning. For instance, in order for children to extend their vocabulary or learn to use language appropriate to different circumstances, your setting needs to create a suitable context for the learning and introduce new words or model different styles of language. Therefore, your setting might set up a 'Garden Centre' role-play area, using new language – 'plants', 'pots', 'compost', 'trowel' and so on – and your practitioners might model instructions on sowing seeds or planting out.

For this important Area of Learning, children need opportunities to:

➤ engage in role-play and other activities where they can listen to others and speak about ideas and events
➤ use language in every aspect of their work and play
➤ enjoy books, rhymes and poems, and find a delight in sounds and words
➤ be immersed in an environment rich in literacy, including books, labels, signs and lists.

To help children's development practitioners should:

➤ value and encourage all forms of communication to help children become confident and 'risk' expressing ideas and feelings
➤ create motivating activities and stimulating areas which encourage speaking, listening, reading and writing
➤ demonstrate how to listen, take turns in speaking, ask questions and share ideas
➤ model new words and different uses of language
➤ encourage children to use language to 'think aloud' and so help them to develop reasoning skills
➤ surround children with language, and plan a wide range of engaging activities where they can practise skills and explore dialogue, reading and writing.

Reception classes need to gradually fashion their language-focused activities to include the literacy hour requirements. The objectives for the literacy hour and the Communication, language and literacy Area of Learning dovetail comfortably together and much of the literacy programme (such as the use of 'big books') is based on best early years practice. Reception classes should introduce elements as discrete activities over time, such as a whole-group sentence writing session linked to an exciting, shared experience. In the last half of the summer term, however, all children should cover full literacy hour lessons – but the component parts should be lively, imaginative and as active as possible with a high level of speaking and listening to reinforce learning, such as using whiteboards and paired discussions.

Mathematical development
This Area of Learning should be developed through a wide range of activities which will enable young children to use and experiment with numbers and engage in counting, sorting, pattern making and matching, comparing and ordering, looking at shapes, space and measures. Mathematical understanding is most appropriately nurtured by your setting using stories, songs and games and imaginative play, to help children enjoy using numbers (including numbers

larger than ten) and to gain confidence. The Stepping Stones in this Area generally give a good framework of skill progression, which will help you plan focused activities for the range of children's ages and stages in your setting.

Mathematical activities need to stem from children's real experience and be concrete and practical. Wise settings will ensure that their whole environment is numerate rich and gives young children an enjoyable context for learning. For example, 'Only four children in the sand-pit' with matching necklaces to be worn, supports counting and one-to-one correspondence easily; cutting wool-lengths to make a puppet's hair supports an awareness of measures, and referring to birthdays, days of the week and session breaks, supports understanding and awareness of time. Children need opportunities to:

➤ play and experiment with resources that encourage mathematical learning, including coins and tills, containers and different-sized toys

➤ enjoy purposeful mathematical role-play, such as setting up a doll's house or sorting toys

➤ participate in games which help them to practise and extend their skills

➤ talk about their counting, patterns, comparisons, shapes and measures.
To maximise children's mathematical learning, practitioners should:

➤ demonstrate a delight in mathematics themselves and encourage positive attitudes through making the learning fun

➤ build in opportunities to extend mathematics in a wide range of other activities

➤ encourage recording in different ways in real contexts (role-play, games, titling pictures and so on) to build children's interest and confidence

➤ plan a programme where there is a proper balance of number, shape and measures, making connections and seeing relationships

➤ make good use of mathematical language at every opportunity

➤ use appropriate mathematical questions (How many? Which is the biggest? How heavy is this one? Are they all the same?)

➤ let children talk about their ideas and encourage them to think deeply (How did you work that out? How do you know? What might come next?)

➤ create a richly numerate environment with interesting and attractive resources

➤ demonstrate to children their own delight and confidence in mathematics!

Reception classes should adopt some of the conventions and ideas from the numeracy strategy programme, but should initially introduce these as separate short activities so as not to overwhelm children.

During the second half of the summer term, however, children should be engaged in the full numeracy session – but settings should plan these with a very heavy emphasis on active participation. Recording work should be closely linked to class themes and related areas wherever possible in order to motivate the children, improve their understanding, and increase their levels of confidence.

Useful tip

Use the 'Audit your provision for Mathematical development' photocopiable sheet on page 99.

Knowledge and understanding of the world

This Area of Learning is concerned with enabling children to develop the knowledge, skills and understanding to make sense of the world. It encompasses work in science, design and technology, history, geography and information and communication technology (ICT). Settings will need to ensure that their curriculum covers all angles with sufficient balance. It will be important for you to look at the programme of themes, topics and play activities you plan to make sure that all aspects have enough emphasis over time. It will be particularly important to look at ways that ICT can be built into work across the curriculum as well as focusing on computer skills. Make good use of the language and mathematical programs, but also let children 'draw/paint' their ideas and recollections, or role-play an office or doctor's surgery.

The Stepping Stones for this Area of Learning can be a guide to progression, but there will be many children who show some of the skills of higher colour bands in some aspects, depending on their previous experience, opportunities and family background. For example, children who enjoy many family excursions may have a more developed awareness of different features in the environment; children with family access to ICT may be very confident keyboard users and some children may have a greater experience of different cultures. Your setting will need to consider carefully how your curriculum and planned activities will ensure all children are assessed, then supported and extended appropriately. You may find the 'Audit your provision for Knowledge and understanding of the world' photocopiable sheet on page 100 helpful.

Children need planned opportunities to:

➤ Have a balanced taste of all aspects of the Area of Learning through first-hand experiences
➤ engage in practical activities which give them a chance to experiment with different tools, materials and resources
➤ explore the immediate local environment and beyond, and handle a range of past and current artefacts
➤ interact with a range of adults, including visitors, and be taught specific skills
➤ gather information from visual materials, artefacts, visitors and from visits.

Practitioners will help learning by:

➤ modelling enthusiastic research and enquiry approaches and using correct technical vocabulary
➤ directly teaching of skills and knowledge, integrated into investigative activities
➤ interacting positively with children and encouraging them to try and to learn from their mistakes productively
➤ using open-ended questions that make children think hard
➤ ensuring all children have equal access to learning, regardless of background, gender and ability

Useful tip

Other resources to employ in this Area of Learning include telephones, tape and video recorders, calculators and 'sat nav' (car satellite navigation systems).

➤ making good use of the outdoors and the local neighbourhood
➤ providing resources that are exciting and sometimes challenging, which stimulate learning
➤ involving parents, carers and visitors in extending children's learning.

Physical development

Physical development is concerned with helping children gain confidence in knowing what they can do and developing a sense of well-being through being physically active, as well as improving their skills of coordination, control, manipulation and movement. It includes all forms of physical activity, both fine and gross motor. It should promote an understanding of a healthy lifestyle. Settings will need to consider how their curriculum covers all of these elements.

You will need to ensure that there are adequate opportunities for children to acquire and refine fine motor coordination skills. They need to have activities which will help them learn how to cut, stick, join, thread, draw, paint and write, using appropriate tools. They need to be encouraged to dress themselves, attend to basic personal hygiene and feed themselves decently. Gross motor activities, both indoor and outdoor, need to be built into schedules, so that children can run, jump, climb, crawl and balance, as well as using and controlling outdoor play vehicles and large- and small-scale play equipment effectively.

The Stepping Stones give an outline progression, but many children will be operating at stages within different colour bands, depending on their earlier experience and out of setting opportunities for Physical development. Practitioners often find very marked differences in confidence and physical expertise in children of the same age. This will need to be reflected in the range of activities you provide. Children will need:

➤ time to develop confidence, learn from mistakes and refine their movements
➤ frequent and regular sessions of taking part in physical activities
➤ opportunities to learn control of their bodies during different activities, using both small and large scale movements
➤ the chance to engage in physical tasks in a safe, interesting, but challenging outdoor environment, exploring the natural world and using a wide range of made resources
➤ encouragement to use and learn through all their senses
➤ opportunities to practise skills and become increasingly independent and responsible.

To support this, practitioners should:

➤ ensure that all children have regular and frequent access to physical activity, indoors and outdoors
➤ create safe spaces, ensuring that clothing is appropriate
➤ include a good range of action rhymes, songs and stories, as well as musical instruments and imaginative props
➤ extend the vocabulary of movement
➤ directly teach safe techniques and skills and insist on proper social conventions
➤ make sure that children have access to a sufficient range of small objects, equipment and materials to handle
➤ determine that all children, including those with mobility difficulty, have access to a good range of physical activities.

Useful tip

The 'Audit your provision for Physical development' photocopiable sheet on page 101 will help you employ good practice in your setting.

Useful tip

Use the 'Audit your provision for Creative development' photocopiable sheet on page 102 to check your setting.

Creative development

Creativity is the bedrock of effective learning, because it enables children to make connections across different elements of learning and extends their understanding. This Area of Learning encompasses art, music, dance, role-play and imaginative play.

Creativity by its nature is essentially practical and dependent on first-hand experience and involvement. This is, of course, the essence of how young children learn best! Children will acquire knowledge, skills and understanding within the area of Creative development but, importantly, Creative development is often the vehicle for further learning – or reinforcement – of other Areas of Learning. Difficult concepts are more easily learned when children are absorbed in activities that are practical, enjoyable and challenging. Study children's faces when they are totally engaged in painting, model-making or playing instruments and see this in action!

The Stepping Stones are a useful guide, but children of the same age may well be operating within elements of different colour bands depending on their prior knowledge and experience.

Children's development is supported best when they:

➤ are surrounded by a rich, colourful and exciting learning environment
➤ know that their creative work is valued
➤ have enough time to explore, experiment and express their ideas – and are able to finish their work
➤ are encouraged to test out ideas and be adventurous
➤ have opportunities to express themselves with all their senses and in all areas of Creative development, and can work on small- and large-scale projects
➤ are introduced to a wide variety of materials, tools, art, music and dance.

To facilitate good learning, practitioners need to:

➤ give children opportunities to develop their own ideas without dominating or over-directing the process
➤ allow children time to experiment and make decisions, particularly about end products or performances, so that the children's own ideas are valued, rather than encouraging replication of an adult's work
➤ create a rich and alluring environment which stimulates curiosity and interest
➤ provide sufficient space – and plan sufficient time – for children to work through creative ideas, refine and improve their work and complete it to their satisfaction
➤ interact sensitively and use open-ended questions to stimulate children's thinking and help them express ideas and develop confidence
➤ provide good quality resources and artefacts and plan opportunities for children to work with artists, musicians, dancers and creative adults
➤ experience the work of a range of artists, craftspeople, musicians, dancers and the creatively acclaimed, through visits, exhibitions, reproductions, recordings and video and artefacts
➤ act as role models in using correct technical vocabulary, demonstrating techniques and discussing and encouraging positive critical evaluation.

Auditing your current provision

The Foundation Stage is recognised as a statutory stage of the National Curriculum for England, alongside Key Stages 1–4 for older pupils. Settings will need to ensure that their curriculum is broad and relevant and that it complies with the requirements for the Foundation Stage, as laid out in the *Curriculum Guidance for the Foundation Stage* (QCA).

OFSTED inspectors, in schools and other settings, will naturally look at your planned programmes and make judgements about their match to these requirements. They will also consider how well the curriculum is implemented in action within your setting and if your provision supports the key elements of the Foundation Stage guidance and promotes young children's learning well. Remember that the *Curriculum Guidance for the Foundation Stage* outlines the Stepping Stones and Early Learning Goals (for settings which receive grant funding and schools with nurseries and Reception-aged children), but it does not prescribe the actual curriculum to achieve these. Rightly, the curriculum design has been left to practitioners to create according to their own clientele and circumstances. There are many different ways to draw up a curriculum and practitioners must decide which is the most suitable for their own settings.

Curriculum organisation styles

Settings frequently organise most of their work within themes and topics, sensibly drawing together work in all six Areas of Learning into a cohesive block. This has the advantage of helping children learn more holistically, and learning can be reinforced across many different linked Areas. Children do not perceive different subject blocks or divisions and, therefore, this is a more natural organisation of learning.

The nature of your setting will generally dictate the type of planning structure you use. Some settings organise their curriculum on a biannual cycle, or even longer if the setting is a unit that children attend for several years. This recognises the necessity of meeting the needs of children of different ages and year groups to ensure that over time, they all experience planned programmes. Others work on an annual cycle of set themes, some covering longer timescales, whilst others are 'mini topics'. Some settings adapt or change their themes and organisation of the curriculum each year as the result of changes in intake or circumstances. Whatever the shape of the curriculum your setting provides, it is important to check that each child will have access to a broad, balanced and purposeful programme – including those children who only attend part-time.

All good settings will want to review the quality and appropriateness of their provision as a necessary part of professional self-review. Practitioners will want to reflect on how successful the different elements of their programmes have been, and how these could be adapted to make learning opportunities even more productive.

Useful tip
Consider the
effectiveness of themes
and topics and question
how these might be
improved:
➤ were themes too
long?
➤ was there sufficient
time?
➤ could local visits be
included?
➤ could play activities
be more relevant and
engaging?
➤ should more
challenging tasks be
planned for some
children?
➤ are resources and the
environment used for
maximum impact?

Checking your provision

OFSTED inspectors will want to know that settings regularly review their curriculum and make alterations based on careful analysis. Even where your evaluation indicates that all is working effectively and no change is needed, you should be able to demonstrate that you have carried out a thorough curriculum examination.

The 'Audit your provision' photocopiable sheets on pages 97–102 give a useful framework for you to audit your current curriculum provision. By progressing systematically through these, you can cover all six Areas of Learning and ensure that your own curriculum supports the required elements. To be of real value, the work should be undertaken over time. Plan to cover one Area of Learning only at a staff meeting and organise it so that all staff can be involved if possible. Where some staff cannot attend, ask them to complete a sheet independently and feed their thoughts into the overall process. You should have all your current planning available – long-, medium- and short-term – and work your way through the questions, jotting down the evidence for good coverage. Aim to spend about an hour on each Area of Learning.

This process will help you identify where elements need to be strengthened, such as where outdoor play activities seem to be rather ordinary and lacking challenge. It should also highlight where some elements may be overlooked or out of balance, such as creative work being generally too directed or very early introduction of the literacy hour in Reception.

Make a note of any adaptations that are deemed necessary and try to prioritise these. If there is an area that needs attention, because it is currently not covered enough or it is out of balance with other Areas of Learning, mark it 'A'. Write 'B' for important areas for attention which can wait until the most urgent ones are addressed, and 'C' for those which may be desirable but are overall less crucial. For example, if your audit reveals that very little outdoor play activities take place, this would be 'A', because it is an essential part of children's learning and a failure to provide opportunities for this vital area of Physical development would impede children's overall progress. However, if regular outdoor play takes place, but activities tend to be limited in challenge and could do with improvement, this might be 'B', because this is important, but is an extension of the programme already in place. 'C' might be that the resources for outdoor play, although generally adequate, would benefit from being updated and expanded.

Start with 'A's and seek ideas for any necessary adaptations to your curriculum themes. Take time to discuss and agree these, then adjust your planning to match. When all the 'A's are done, agree how to tackle the rest over time.

Matching your curriculum to your children's needs

What makes your setting unique and special?

It is important that you have built a curriculum that covers the six Areas of Learning thoroughly, using the QCA document *Curriculum Guidance for the Foundation Stage*, but settings have scope to determine the content of their programmes. You need to be sure your curriculum highlights 'inclusion' and that no children are unnecessarily disadvantaged in their learning.

Every setting is unique. You should consider the nature of your intake, so you determine the emphasis you place on the different aspects of the six

Areas of Learning. Your setting might serve a very settled area, or one where parents/carers have a more transitory pattern of movement. Most, or few, of your parents/carers may work outside the home. There may be high levels of unemployment or changing working patterns locally. You may draw children from a wide area and from many different backgrounds. Perhaps most of the parents/carers work and your daily contact is with other adults who care for the children. These factors need consideration when you are tailoring learning experiences to your intake. Consider how you will communicate your curriculum content to parents/carers and involve them in their children's learning.

Cultural and religious backgrounds

Children may come from many different cultural backgrounds or from predominantly only one or two. You need to consider the implications for your curriculum. The rich diversity of your intake could present wonderful opportunities to involve the parents/carers and give your children real experiences in cultural activities, and this should be reflected in your curriculum. For example, if you have Hindu families, you can build Divali celebrations into your autumn term programmes.

However, you may have few children from different cultural backgrounds. Your curriculum should offer opportunities for children to respect people's different cultures and beliefs within Personal, social and emotional development. Topics need to reflect a culturally diverse society and there are implications for your choice of home-play areas, resources and general activities. A topic on 'Holidays', for example, could give valuable opportunities to look at the similarities and differences in people's lifestyles, costumes and artefacts. Home-play areas could include a range of appropriate dressing-up clothes and everyday items, and a local market visit might give children a chance to look at different produce from other lands.

English as an additional language

Your setting might include children from backgrounds where English is not the mother tongue. Even where parents and carers speak English well, there can be important factors to consider. Some children may not hear English spoken at home, whereas for others this will be the norm.

Where young children are learning English as an additional language there are curriculum implications. There should be high levels of adult interaction in carefully planned language-focused activities. The mother tongue should also be valued – children may be achieving well in their first language! The curriculum could include opportunities for all children to learn a nursery rhyme or a few words of greeting in different languages. Planned deployment of support staff (with special training sessions) would help, and also involving bilingual parents/carers to support children. This might include being alongside children during physical activities, stressing the words for 'up', 'down', 'over', 'under', 'forwards', 'backwards' and so on, in both languages.

Social backgrounds

Children may be from advantaged or socially-deprived areas, or there could be a wide range. Your intake may be fortunate enough to engage in family trips to interesting places, have access to computers at home and visit the local library. Other children may have little stimulation outside the activities you offer them. If so, you need to create a programme of local walks, such as to a park and library facility. You will need to plan for time to explore computers and provide

Useful tip

If you have Muslim children, consult their parents about annual dates for Eid celebrations.

interesting visitors and stimulating experiences, which help fill some of the identified gaps.

Children may come from homes where there is little chance to play outside and/or alongside other children. Where this is the case, their gross motor development may be limited. Your curriculum should then include an extensive programme of climbing, balancing, pedalling and so on, to help children's development. In fastidious homes children have too few opportunities to use scissors, paint, glue and generally engage in 'messy' activities! This knowledge will help you plan group activities to develop children's freedom to experiment without constraint.

Varying year groups

Even within a setting, different cohorts of children may present very differently year on year. For example, there may be year groups where the boys seriously outnumber the girls. Sometimes the local demography (such as the opening of a new housing development or changes to local housing policies) results in a large influx of new children or temporarily diminishing numbers. Occasionally, even within an age group, many children's birthdays fall very close together and this results in an uneven spread of admission numbers.

Varying abilities

Some years contain a larger number of children with special needs than others. Your initial entry assessment will help you highlight those areas where more focus needs to be planned into your programme. In school settings the *Foundation Stage Profile* will indicate those areas in which most children attain well, plus those that need greater attention. You need to consider the background and experience of your children carefully and use this information to plan your programmes, so that you do not miss an opportunity to meet your intakes' needs as fully as possible.

Planning for special educational needs (SEN)

Early years practitioners have a vital role in both the early identification of children with special needs and also the carefully planned support for those children who have recognised special educational needs. They are frequently the first people to observe children in an educational setting and observe how they cope and react with learning experiences outside the home. They also have a crucial role in establishing productive partnerships with parents and carers and in helping them know how they can support their children's learning best. Sometimes this role has a very sensitive dimension, helping parents and carers to come to accept the term 'special educational needs' as it relates to their children in a positive and supportive way.

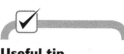

Useful tip
The 'What makes our setting unique' photocopiable sheet on page 103 is designed to help you identify the particular needs of your children.

Non-school settings

In non-school settings it is essential that a member of staff has overall lead as special needs coordinator and guides the rest of the staff. They need a good understanding of the setting's role in identifying children with potential learning difficulties and aiding staff to meet their needs in the best way they can. It is important that they help all staff know how to identify children with possible special educational needs and develop a process to track children's progress. They need to familiarise themselves with the SEN *Code of Practice* requirements relating to early years settings and the specific local arrangements for referrals and obtaining support from a range of local agencies, such as the local health service. Teacher mentors can be very helpful links for LEA procedures.

School-based settings

In school settings, there should be an overall special educational needs coordinator (SENCO) in post, who has responsibility for overseeing the special needs provision. However, such staff may be based predominantly with older children. In these cases, the SENCO will need to liaise closely with the Foundation Stage phase and will also need to rely heavily on the knowledge and expertise of early years staff.

Identifying potential special educational needs

If your setting is the first placement that a young child has enjoyed, early observations may alert you to some specific learning difficulties that may be encountered. Alternatively, some initial concerns may have been raised during induction visits or through discussions with parents and carers. Some parents/carers may raise the issue with you, feeling that their child may have special educational needs, but being unsure. Many first-time parents, because of demographic work patterns, do not have extended family members to ask about child development.

The quality of your observations will be a key factor in identifying the nature of a child's apparent difficulties and deciding whether support is required through Early Years Action within your setting. It will be important that arrangements are put into place, which allow all staff to contribute to discussions about each child's settling into the setting and their general stage of development. This can be done by establishing a rolling programme where all children are reviewed in turn, focusing on just one or two children each session, and getting all staff to contribute their observations over a range of different activities.

Where children may be giving staff some cause for concern, it will be important to plan very focused activities where there is a high level of staff interaction and where children can be closely observed. These activities will need to be planned and revisited over time, so that judgements are secure. This will help determine the difference between a child's natural but marginally slower rate of maturation or past limited experiences affecting responses, against general learning difficulties.

Planning support programmes

If a child has transferred from another setting, or has had referral from other agencies, you should have very useful information on their progress and SEN. If not, you have your own observations and discussions with parents/carers as a basis for initial assessment.

Useful tip
Careful, considered planning will help you support special needs manageably through adjusting elements of your current provision.

You will need to create an assessment, planning and review cycle to include:

➤ an initial assessment of a child's rate of progress, specific difficulties and needs
➤ what will be planned to help the child make progress
➤ regular reviews to check how well support is working.
  You will then need to consider:

➤ how the child will be taught at different times and who will do this
➤ who will be the key member of staff to oversee continuity, review progress and collate information
➤ how support staff will be deployed to meet the child's needs
➤ how parents, carers, helpers and specialist advisers will be involved
➤ how the curriculum and everyday programmes will be adapted to meet the child's needs
➤ which teaching strategies and approaches will optimise the child's progress and help them fulfil their potential.

Checklist

➤ The key test for further action to meet SEN is evidence that the current rate of progress is inadequate.
➤ It should not be assumed that all children will progress at the same rate.
➤ Children must not be regarded as having a learning difficulty solely because the language, or forms of language, of their home is different from the language in which they are taught.

It will be vital to collate observations and examples of a child's reactions and work to help diagnose particular areas for specific attention. This will be especially true if the child has considerable learning difficulties and needs to be identified for Early Years Action Plus, where the specialist help and support of other agencies is required.

Using vital local resources

Part of the uniqueness of your setting will be its place within the local community and the surrounding environment. Every setting has access to a variety of local resources which can be drawn upon. Do not despair if, at first glance, these seem limited. Not all settings have the advantages of nearby museums or parks, and rural settings may feel removed from access to more sophisticated urban resources. However, with some imagination and a little team effort, many very useful resources can be found.

It will be useful for you to set aside about half an hour for staff to go through the 'Maximising our unique local resources' photocopiable sheet on page 104 to review possibilities. Undertake this as a whole group. First, go through each section identifying all local features which might be available to your setting. Then address each one and list, on separate sheets, how each feature could be used in future. At the end of the activity you should have several exciting areas to explore!

Take time to consider the following questions:
- ➤ what contacts do we have?
- ➤ how could we make contact?
- ➤ would a visit be useful?
- ➤ could we encourage a visitor from there?
- ➤ what special skills, ideas or areas of interest might visitors have?
- ➤ how might this enrich the curriculum?
- ➤ are there any resources they could give?
- ➤ are there any sponsorship opportunities?
- ➤ how can this be planned into programmes?
- ➤ how should this be followed up?

Case study

In a rather heavily industrialised area, a setting was keen to help their children have a real experience of growing things. So a nursery-class teacher wrote to the manager of a nearby garden centre and made an appointment to see him. She took some examples of children's paintings of flowers, complete with their scribed sentences to show the children's work. The manager was keen to display these! She spoke about her setting, the lack of green spaces and showed him photographs of their limited outdoor area. The teacher received a guided tour of the 'backroom' activities and the public areas. She asked to bring groups of children and whether there were particular times of the year when this would be especially interesting and easy for the garden centre to manage. Arrangements were made for a visit in the autumn when the bulbs were displayed. Centre staff showed children the different kinds of bulbs and how to plant these up for Christmas flowering, and everyone prepared their own. (Photographs were taken and sent to the local press to give the centre some good publicity!) Just before Christmas, the manager visited the setting to look at the children's bulbs, talk about Christmas at the garden centre and to bring some different examples of flowering plants.

Ideas

- ➤ Ask a local librarian to visit and read favourite stories.
- ➤ Have a clinic or dental nurse talk about a hygiene and health area.
- ➤ Ask the clinic, practices or vets for leaflets and old, clean resources for a role-play area.
- ➤ Go to the Post Office and send letters to Father Christmas.
- ➤ Visit a building such as a local church to look at wood, metal, stone, glass and fabric crafts.
- ➤ Make links with a local factory or large supermarket and ask for resources for play areas and for personnel to come to talk about what they do.
- ➤ Invite ambulance, police and fire-brigade staff to come in uniform and demonstrate some of their work.
- ➤ Ask community and religious leaders to bring in artefacts and show how they celebrate different festivals (for example, Divali, Hanukkah, Eid, Ash Wednesday).

Tapping into local talent

In every community, there will be special interest clubs, societies and service organisations. You can find out about the range of provision in your area, as well as discovering contacts for the different groups, by enquiring at the local library. You can also scan posters of fund-raising events and use contact numbers from these. Additionally, you can write to local newspapers to follow up articles and pictures from different clubs that have been featured.

Members of these groups can be a rich source of support and can add to your curriculum provision. Service organisations (such as the Rotary, Round Table, Inner Wheel, Lions and so on) are often keen to serve their local community and can offer help with transport, contribute funds for equipment, subsidise travel and visits costs, and they will frequently offer extra adults to accompany parties or come into settings to help out.

Many settings have used members of local handicraft, painting, gardening and photography clubs to share their hobbies and skills with young children. One local horticultural club earmarked a section of an allotment and worked with children to prepare the plot, plant and tend crops. A water-colour painting society taught small groups of children and organised an exhibition of their work alongside club members' own art at the town hall. A sewing group came into a Reception class regularly and made multicultural dressing-up clothes, soft furnishings for the home-play area and costumes for the Christmas concert based on the children's own drawn designs.

The planning cycle and systems

There is no one, approved way of planning your curriculum! However, careful planning is essential to ensure that children's learning is effective, exciting, imaginative, engaging and progressive. This is particularly important in settings where there is more than one age group, to ensure that all children are

challenged at the right level, so they can make the rate of progress they should.

Planning is needed to ensure that all six Areas of Learning in the Foundation Stage are given equal emphasis. Each Area also needs to be balanced, with all aspects of learning within each Area covered and revisited regularly and frequently, so that children can acquire, practise and improve skills and knowledge in a systematic way. Good planning enables practitioners to build up a bank of knowledge about each child and how they learn best, building on both children's interests and needs, and programming a range of appropriate activities to support their development. The planning process works most effectively when all practitioners working in the setting are involved – contributing ideas, taking a lead on different aspects and fully understanding the learning purposes behind planned activities.

Planning should be written in a consistent format, so it can be easily shared with others (both within the setting and those with a legitimate interest, for example, OFSTED inspectors). It can be useful for a reference for further planning, forming an outline of activities that can be adapted and refined in the light of experience, or for very different cohorts of children. You may find the 'Long-, Medium- and Short-term planning grid' photocopiable sheets on pages 105–107 to be a helpful resource.

Long-term planning

Some settings will have children who attend for a relatively short time, whereas others may have children attending for two years or more. Some settings offer full-time provision, in others attendance may be part-time or a mixture of the two. Practitioners will want to cater for the needs of their children appropriately, enabling them to cover the six Areas of Learning fully and ensuring that as they grow older, children have more challenging tasks that help them make the progress they should.

A long-term plan is needed to help you have a clear pathway for one or two years ahead. It should set out in broad terms what you want the children to learn and how you will organise this over time. It will help you check that all six Areas of Learning are adequately emphasised. It will give you a good overall framework for coverage.

Long-term plans are generally designed to plot the learning experience pathway for whole groups of children. This does not mean that you cannot follow some occasional exciting opportunity to extend learning that was not initially planned for, such as a chance to arrange a theatre visit to a suitable show, host unexpected visitors from another country or have a wonderful time exploring a heavy snowfall! Those magical events can be built into your short-term planning and you can enjoy them and then later revert to the overall plan, with some time adjustments if necessary.

Your long-term planning should take account of your setting's pattern. If you only have children with a limited age range, say four-year-olds, a one-year plan would be ideal to give an overview of the range of learning opportunities that will be offered. If you have children attending for two years, commonly three- and four-year-olds, a two-year planning cycle would be most appropriate.

Medium-term planning

Although *Planning for Learning in the Foundation Stage* (QCA) recognises that many practitioners find long-term and short-term planning sufficient, you may find it helpful to draw up medium-term plans which bridge the gap between these layers. Building in a simple medium-term plan enables settings to organise the different elements from their overall long-term plan into termly or half-termly manageable chunks. Medium-term planning is generally concerned with whole groups of children and it can be useful to highlight the specific needs of identified groups, for example, induction for new cohorts, or the gradual introduction of the literacy hour for Reception-class children.

The time available may differ from year to year (depending on Easter or other variables), and what fits into a Spring term one year may need to be changed the next. It also allows practitioners to decide to cover one or two planned elements at different times of the year than in the original plans, if this seems a better arrangement, without losing out on the overall coverage. For settings running two-year plans, it is hard to hold the different planning in your head for such a long period, and medium-term plans will help you look at smaller portions more easily.

Short-term planning

A short-term plan derives from the medium-term plan, or directly from the long-term planning if no medium-term plan is used. It needs to be developed using practitioners' ongoing observation and informal assessment of the children, so that it is designed to meet their needs and extend their learning. Short-term planning is usually concerned with individual or targeted groups of children in mind. It should be used to identify where individual children, or named groups, will have staff-directed activities and where there will be opportunities for free-choice or self-directed work. Observations of children will help you adjust your short-term plans to meet their needs and, importantly, you are able to maximise the learning from unexpected events, especially those that are child-initiated.

It can be drawn up on a daily or weekly basis, although a weekly system is probably a more manageable process for most settings. It is generally easier to timetable one regular weekly planning session, which most practitioners can attend, than to schedule daily sessions. Weekly planning can give practitioners more time to gather or make resources, brief helpers and visitors, prepare specific activities and arrange areas of the accommodation. However, settings that have the time and staff to meet and plan for each day ahead may feel comfortable with this daily approach.

Planning for themes and topics

Many settings find it useful to plan their work under broad themes. This gives the advantage of providing a holistic framework with interrelated parts. Young children do not learn in compartmentalised units, and what they learn is dependent on the experiences they encounter. So themes and topics provide a good way of reinforcing learning through activities that are linked and where learning can be cross-referenced. A topic approach is an excellent way of involving parents/carers, who can support learning out of the setting with related visits and activities.

Typically, settings plan topics for half-term periods, sometimes even a whole term, but this is not necessary. The time allocated should match the nature of the topic. Therefore, some topics could run for a long period whilst others, such as seasonal topics (for example, Bonfire Night), could be mini-topics of short duration. A whole term devoted to one topic is probably too long. Interest could wane or Areas of Learning become unbalanced, unless there are frequent changes of emphasis, which make it a series of different topics related to one theme.

It is also possible to have more than one topic running concurrently. This could comprise an overarching theme, such as 'Our town', with clearly defined Areas of Learning, supplemented by smaller topics. For example, a setting may take advantage of a chance to be involved in a local initiative (a visiting theatre group or links with another provider) and free-standing, shorter topics can be run alongside the main one. However, care must be taken to ensure that all Areas of Learning over time have proper attention and that the programme is not overcrowded. Some content pruning may be necessary to ensure quality, unpressured coverage!

Useful tip

➤ Review your topic choices regularly to keep them fresh.

➤ Check each Area of Learning carefully within each topic and ensure that all the elements within each of the six Areas are well balanced.

Planning for play

Well-planned play is the bedrock of young children's learning. Through carefully planned play, indoors and outdoors, children can learn how to make sense of the world in a pleasurable and engaging way.

Children need to be able to:

➤ explore, investigate and learn about their environment and different materials, artefacts and circumstances
➤ practise and develop concepts, ideas and skills
➤ learn how to operate within set rules and control their behaviour accordingly
➤ work individually, alongside others and cooperatively
➤ experiment, take risks and make mistakes which they can learn from
➤ work creatively and extend their imagination
➤ solve problems and communicate their reasoning and ideas
➤ work through fears or anxieties within a safe situation.

All these elements are best served through play and practitioners should plan carefully to provide opportunities for quality play activities. Go through your long-term planning and identify specific areas and themes where play can be emphasised.

Ideas

➤ Create a stimulating new environment indoors by altering the layout to match a theme (for example, an undersea world, rainbow rooms, or around the world).
➤ Devise an imaginative outdoor area (for example, a 'Gingerbread house', or a wild terrain).
➤ Identify a specific play area (a fire station, campsite and so on).
➤ Establish resources to stimulate play activities (including dressing-up clothes, animal masks, gardening equipment, multicultural home artefacts).

Transfer your ideas in broad detail to your medium-term planning and, ultimately, in more detail to your short-term planning. Review your planning and make sure that there are real opportunities for children to engage in play each session if possible. Check from time to time that individual children have been actively involved in a range of different play situations.

Frequently the setting up of imaginative and irresistible areas will stimulate children's spontaneous play ideas. Children will often adapt resources to create their own exciting play worlds. Be prepared to adapt short-term planning to follow an exciting unexpected event or opportunity. For instance, the arrival of a new baby could trigger many wonderful chances for your setting to focus on change and growth and set up 'baby care' play. This would help any older child work through any anxieties about a new sibling and also provide an engaging area for all children's learning.

Useful tip

The 'Long-, Medium- and Short-term planning grid' photocopiable sheets on pages 105–107 will help you successfully plan play activities.

Case study

In a nursery school a practitioner read a book to the children about a dinosaur searching for a safe place to lay her eggs. This delighted the group, who then enjoyed playing with a range of plastic dinosaur models. The next morning a girl announced that she wanted to make a nest for a dinosaur. The teacher skilfully questioned her to stimulate her imagination and extend her learning and the girl searched for a container and found some pets' bedding straw to go in it. With guidance she decided to build a woodblock cave and enlisted two friends to help her. As they built, they referred to the book for ideas. At home time the structure was left with the dinosaur on the nest.

Staff wanted to promote further play and learning, so they obtained an empty eggshell and slid a tiny dinosaur model inside, leaving it for the girl to find next morning. Joyfully the children discovered the 'baby' and, as a group, played spontaneously, acting out the dinosaurs' adventures – which staff later scribed into a storybook.

Using staff effectively

Any setting's greatest resource is its staff. Everyone who works in a setting with young children, and has a background in early years practice, has significant experience and ideas to contribute to the planning process.

The range of staff employed in different settings is vast. There will be teachers, nursery nurses with NNEB qualifications and staff with BTechs and NVQs. Some will have experience in school settings, others in many different settings, or perhaps just one sector. The training of staff will also have difference emphases. Teachers will have covered a broad course including child development, learning theory and psychology, whereas others may have had a more defined focus on childcare. All need to be included in the planning process, so that the best ideas are gleaned and everyone knows clearly what the teaching programmes will be and their role within them. The best settings, with the most effective practice, always have a strong team identity. A key feature of their success is that individuals bring their special talents, interests and skills to enrich the whole provision, working in a cooperative and collaborative manner.

The leadership role

It is generally advisable for one person to take the lead and act as coordinator. Occasionally this could be a shared role, with two practitioners working together. In a few settings the leadership role is rotated. All practitioners are busy, so the leader should break the back of any review of planning by being well prepared and with options and ideas to present to the rest of the team.

The lead coordinator should:

➤ be thoroughly familiar with the requirements of the Foundation Stage curriculum and the supplementary *Planning for Learning in the Foundation Stage* materials.
➤ look at the examples of curriculum planning in the publication and consider if there is anything that the setting could beneficially adopt
➤ seek out planning models from other settings and consider their usefulness (this might include asking a teacher mentor for suggestions, or contacting nearby settings and arranging a planning 'swap shop and tea' sharing session)

➤ lead planning review meetings in the setting, suggesting possible improvements to planning, or the adoption of a more useful and manageable style

➤ decide the timescales and planning cycle for your long-term, medium-term (if you use this) and short-term planning and set diary dates. For example, review and content update of long-term plans – May (two meetings); development of medium-term plans, ready for September start – June (two meetings); weekly short-term planning meetings – Thursdays 3.30– 4.30pm (with all staff)

➤ set up and run the review meetings

➤ demonstrate that all team members are valued and actively seek their views

➤ monitor the arrangements as they run, consult with the team and suggest any alterations as necessary.

Involving support staff

Find out about the interests and skills your staff have. You could do this in a fun quiz way, asking staff to complete a sheet for themselves, using the example, (right), as a guide.

Redistribute the quiz sheets and get staff to read out someone else's answers. You might get some insight into ways that your staff can have opportunities to use their skills or develop ideas that can benefit your setting. For example, in one setting a nursery nurse with a secret passion for gardening took a lead in creating a garden area and led the planning of a topic based on this. It is essential to find a way that support staff can be part of planning discussions. This can be difficult if they are part-time or have unusual hours. However, with considerable advanced warning, and the leader stressing the importance of their views, it might be possible for them to make special arrangements.

Staff quiz

I think I'm good at

I really enjoy

Interests, talents, hobbies OUTSIDE work

Something few people know about me

Given the chance, I would love to

In our setting, I'd like to be more involved in

For whole-team long- and medium-term planning and reviews

Consider these different arrangements currently in use.

➤ Build in a whole-team day when the setting is closed, have a tight agenda to review and plan – and ensure that you all enjoy some delicious refreshments.

➤ If a whole day is difficult, arrange meetings during two separate half-day closures – one morning, one afternoon – which may be easier to cover.

➤ In school settings, ask the head teacher early to plan in a Foundation Stage staff planning day, or two part-days, out of the allocated INSET days. Many settings have half a day in September at the beginning of term, with half a day later in the year by negotiation.

➤ Build in a series of hour-long staff meetings on different days of the week, after hours and cover the planning in 'bite-sized chunks'.

➤ Have an evening session from 3.30–6.30pm and then all go for a meal together!

Short-term planning sessions

These are vital for the quality of your programmes. Everyone needs to know what they are to do and how children's learning is to be maximised. Staff need to know how particular children will be supported, challenged and assessed by them and they need to know any responsibilities they have for setting up specific activities or displays, for example, decorating the classroom at different times of year.

➤ Set up a regular weekly time when all staff can be together, or if unavoidable, meet early in the week and pass on proposed planning to part-timers for comment.

➤ Thursdays are useful for planning as staff have a day to gather resources and any materials they may need to prepare activities for the following week.

➤ Lunchtime meetings can be useful, but time is usually limited. Consider sessions after work – some settings plan fortnightly programmes to maximise time.

➤ Keep meetings brisk and make every second count, but make sure everyone knows their personal schedule for the following week!

Chapter 2 Planning assessment into the curriculum

> ➤ **Linking assessment opportunities into your curriculum**
> ➤ **The assessment cycle**
> ➤ **Special needs issues**
> ➤ **Issues for Reception classes**
> ➤ **Dealing with the** *Foundation Stage Profile*
> ➤ **Assessment and issues for other settings**

Linking assessment opportunities into your curriculum

Good early years practitioners have always assessed children. It has been established good practice for practitioners to make a basic assessment of each child's stage of development at their commencement at any setting, although this may not have been carried out in a formal manner. Such initial assessments have enabled practitioners to plan activities that properly support children's development step by step. A child who has limited fine motor control and finds pencil skills difficult, may be encouraged to develop improved manipulative skills by engaging in specific activities, such as dot-to-dot drawing, tracing or pattern making. Another child, who joins a setting already able to read some simple texts, will need more challenging language activities and needs encouragement to acquire phonic skills.

Skilled early years staff constantly, and almost automatically, observe the reactions and responses of children in many different situations. In this way they quickly begin to make judgements about individual children's progress. In the most effective settings, time is set aside for all staff, both teaching and support, to contribute their observations towards an overall assessment of each child's development. By sharing observations and evidence for children's progress, most practitioners will gradually acquire a clear picture to help general assessment. However, some assessments need to be made with rather more precision and detail and cannot necessarily be left to chance observations. For example, if certain activities are only covered occasionally, it would be all too easy to miss some children's reactions and staff may find it difficult to recall or assess their progress overall. This will be especially true for Reception classes, where judgements for the *Foundation Stage Profile* in each of the 13 assessment scales (each of which has nine specific points) will need to be made for each child by the end of the summer term. More detailed advice on this issue will be given later in this chapter.

Recognising assessment opportunities
How can we build on the random nature of observation and assessment? Build more precise assessment into your normal curriculum.
➤ If possible, have six different-coloured highlighter pens and select one for each Area of Learning.

➤   Go through your long-term planning for each of the six Areas of Learning. Mark with the appropriate highlighter those activities that may be infrequent or occasional, but where assessment would be useful (for example, a visit to a mosque, music-making activities, phonic work, calculating).

➤   Ensure that, when long-term plans are organised into medium- and short-term planning, the highlighting system alerts practitioners to make arrangements for observation and assessment. Add the appropriate highlighter to the relevant weekly planned sections.

➤   Then decide how to set up suitable activities where children will be observed. These activities should be your normal curriculum content; you do not need to set up a special task.

➤   Decide which children are to be observed and devise groups that will be directed to the activity at times when named personnel will be present to make the assessments and note significant issues.

➤   Additionally, agree if there are any other areas where observations should be more formally undertaken that week. However, be careful not to overload the observations and limit the freedom of staff to interact with children.

Preventing assessment overload

Assessments should be carried out in the course of normal work and no one should be expected to expend extra energy devising an unwieldy set of assessment tasks. Rather, it should require an awareness of which activities will provide the best information to observers. As a rough guide, and to keep assessment in a manageable perspective, do not have more than two 'formal' assessments each day. In part-time settings, only one assessment observation per session at the most is really manageable. Many very effective settings restrict their observed assessments to only two or three each week and still build up a valuable bank of first-hand judgements. Obviously, staff who are formally observing cannot be involved in any other activities in the setting at that time, so excessive numbers of assessments greatly reduce the quality of adult to child interactions!

Preparing staff

It will be useful for all staff to share observation techniques and ideas together, so that everyone is aware of what is expected, what to look out for and how to record their findings. Devise a standard observation/assessment form to record the observer's notes. You may find it helpful to use the 'Learning objectives assessment form' photocopiable sheet on page 108.

Ask volunteers to carry out some preliminary observations and to fill in the forms. Circulate copies and ask all staff to look at these together. Discuss the content and judgements and the issues of carrying out thorough observations. This will help your setting streamline your system. When all staff have had observation experience you may wish to adapt the form to suit your setting's preference and house style! You will also find more guidance on productive day-to-day assessment in Chapter 4.

Useful tip

You may need to plan 'revisit' tasks and activities, so that you can assess how certain children have developed and acquired skills and understanding as they mature.

The assessment cycle

It is useful for settings to remind themselves of the key to successful assessment systems, as defined on page 24 of the *Curriculum Guidance for the Foundation Stage* (QCA).

Principles for early years education

Practitioners must be able to observe and respond appropriately to children. This principle requires practitioners to observe children and respond appropriately to help them make progress. This is demonstrated when practitioners:

➤ make systematic observations and assessments of each child's achievements, interests and learning styles
➤ use these observations and assessments to identify learning priorities and plan relevant and motivating learning experiences for each child
➤ match their observations to the expectations of the Early Learning Goals.

Assessment is done for the vital purpose of tracking each child's progress in learning and then presenting the child with the next steps in their learning experience. Assessment should not become a paper exercise, nor dominate any setting's provision. It should be seen as a tool for analysis of any child's learning to date, from which professional judgements about planning the appropriate future activities, experiences and direct adult interventions for that child's development should stem.

Beginning the assessment process and cycle

For many settings, the assessment cycle will start with the first contact with parents and carers. In school settings this could also be the case, but they may have some valuable early assessment information that has been gathered at a previous setting or, in some cases, from the involvement of other agencies.

Every setting needs to be clear about the range of available information, how this can be obtained and how this can be absorbed into their own systems. No information should be disregarded, even though settings will obviously wish to make their own judgements on children's entry stage of development and how they present in a new environment.

There can be many permutations:

➤ children come from a single previous setting
➤ children come from many different earlier settings and some have never been at another setting
➤ few, or no, children have any earlier setting experience
➤ some have had specialist early provision because of special educational needs
➤ some have had support from one, or several, different outside agencies.

Useful tip

You may find 'Our assessment cycle planner' photocopiable sheet on page 109 helpful in developing the most manageable and appropriate programme for your setting.

Consider following the six steps to assessment success!

Step 1 – Gathering previous information

Determine the intake experience of your children. Where children have had previous experience it will be useful to contact the different providers with a standard request letter, suitably personalised to your own setting, and ask them to pass on any assessment information. Take particular note of any special educational needs information and consider how you will use this for the benefit of identified children. Bear in mind that all settings may not keep formal records, so if possible arrange to make a personal visit to discuss individual children. Alternatively, send a very simple, user-friendly form and gently persuade staff to complete it for you!

Step 2 – First parent/carer contact

Most settings will arrange to meet parents and carers. This may be done by home visits, invitations to accompany their child to your setting, parent/carer individual discussions, or a combination of these approaches. You will need to work out what kind of information you should glean at this time and how you will record it. (Chapter 3 'Manageable assessment systems' may help you.)

Step 3 – First admission

Many settings will admit new children on a phased or rolling programme, sensibly admitting only a few children at a time in order to give the new children as much attention as possible. It is useful to appoint a key adult to support each new child and make some preliminary observations about their stage of development.

Step 4 – After settling

Young children often need time to settle into a new environment and feel confident. You will get a more accurate indication of a child's stage of development after a period of three weeks or so. Observations made now can be compared with any earlier information you received prior to admission. You could also meet with parents/carers and discuss your initial observations and share their views. This should also give you an excellent opportunity to forge productive relationships.

Step 5 – Regular, timed progress checks

Decide the timescales for these checks and who will be responsible for observing, collating and recording all significant information, and how this will be shared with parents/carers. Checks could be done on a half-termly basis, or on a rolling programme of, say, two identified children being observed each session (the overall timescale would vary depending on your setting's population, but realistically, on an intake of 30 part-timers, would take around three weeks), or at the end, or at key junctures, of each topic covered. Work from the key assessment times you have identified in your curriculum and ensure that children are observed and assessed working at suitable activities.

Step 6 – Summative assessment

Towards the end of each child's time in your setting, use all the assessment information you have gathered to draw together an overall series of judgements linked to all six Areas of Learning. Use the *Foundation Stage Profile* to record all the necessary elements, if appropriate, or a compatible proforma, personal to your setting. Please see Chapter 5 'Effective recording' for further guidance.

Special needs issues

Practitioners will need to plan for all children's learning, including those children who require extra support or have identified educational needs or disabilities. The emphasis should be twofold. Firstly, to remove any barriers to learning where these exist (for example, ensuring disabled children have access to the full programme of learning experiences, including physical activities). Secondly, to prevent learning difficulties from developing, by assessing children and providing carefully tailored learning activities which support children of different abilities and stages of development.

Early years practitioners have a vital part to play in building and then working in a productive partnership with parents/carers. They need to use their professional expertise to identify individual children's learning needs and then to respond rapidly with strategies to help these children progress well.

Every setting needs to have a member of staff, who is identified as having particular responsibility for overseeing SEN concerns. Settings are charged with the responsibility of identifying children who need extra support with their learning for Early Years Action, and then to draw up practical Individual Education Plans (IEPs) to guide staff on how to meet their needs. Settings also need to track their progress very precisely. For those children who need more support than a setting can provide, particularly specialist help, practitioners must be aware of the requirements of Early Years Action Plus and the need to make careful observations and assessments to inform any decisions about the nature of further support.

In some cases, children joining your setting will have already been identified as requiring additional support by previous providers or through other agencies, such as the Health Service. These children may already have IEPs or even Statements of educational need, and you will need to assimilate any stipulated requirements into your own support, track progress carefully and be prepared to report on developments at regular reviews.

Identifying children with special educational needs in your setting

There should not be an assumption that all children will progress at the same rate. Young children have different maturation rates and their past experiences will play a part in the speed of further development. Young children frequently learn in bursts, and respond with different levels of interest and application to different types of learning activity.

In particular, children should not be regarded as having a learning difficulty solely because their home language, or forms of language, is different from the language in which they are taught.

The key test for identifying children with potential SEN, and where further action is necessary by the setting, is to provide definite evidence that their current rate of progress is inadequate.

Settings need to conform to the requirements laid out in the SEN *Code of Practice* and Section 6 of *The SEN Toolkit* (both available from DfES publications, PO Box 5050, Sherwood Park, Annesley, Nottingham, NG15 0DJ. Telephone: 0845 6022260).

The SEN Code of Practice
The broad principles of the *Code* are that:

➤ a child with SEN should have their needs met
➤ the SEN of children will normally be met in mainstream schools or settings
➤ the views of the child should be sought and taken into account
➤ parents/carers have a vital role in supporting their child's education
➤ children with SEN should be offered full access to a broad, balanced and relevant education, including an appropriate curriculum for the Foundation Stage and National Curriculum.

Critical success factors for any setting – the ten commandments!
1 The culture, practice, management and deployment of resources within the setting must be designed to ensure that all the children's needs are met.
2 Local education authorities and settings need to work together to ensure that children's special educational needs are identified early.
3 Local education authorities and settings need to exploit best practice when devising support and interventions.
4 Practitioners should take into account the wishes of the child according to their age and understanding.
5 Professionals and parents/carers need to work in partnership for the benefit of the children.
6 Parents'/carers' views regarding their child's particular needs must be taken into account.
7 The impact of each intervention must be regularly reviewed, as must the child's overall progress
8 There must be close cooperation with all agencies and a multi-disciplinary approach must be taken
9 Local education authorities must make assessments within prescribed time limits.
10 Where local education authorities agree Statements, these must always be clear and detailed.

Early Years Action
Triggers for practitioners' concern and possible classification of a child are:

➤ the child makes little or no progress despite your targeted approaches
➤ the child continues to work at levels below those expected for their age
➤ the child has persistent emotional and/or behavioural problems, which are not ameliorated by your setting's approaches
➤ the child has sensory/physical problems and makes poor progress despite special aids
➤ the child has communication problems and requires individual intervention in order to learn.

Early Years Action Plus

This is characterised by the involvement of external support agencies, which help settings with advice on IEPs and targets, give specialist assessments and may give extra support. This varies according to local policies. Likely triggers are:

➤ the child makes little or no progress over a long period
➤ the child works at a level substantially below that expected for their age
➤ the child has emotional/behavioural difficulties that substantially interfere with their own and others' learning, despite your help
➤ the child has sensory/physical needs requiring help from a specialist service
➤ the child has communication difficulties that form a substantial barrier to learning.

Nursery issues and establishing good 'Value Added'

The introduction of the Foundation Stage as a phase in its own right, in September 2000, was widely and rightly welcomed by early years practitioners. It gave long overdue recognition to the vital early learning and formative experiences that were provided by good quality early years settings.

At this time, children entering primary school were assessed against key elements of the six Areas of Learning by the use of a statutory Baseline Assessment. However, although all schools had to complete a Baseline Assessment, they could choose which 'approved Baseline Assessment' format they used, usually following their own local education authority version or one recommended by local advisers. The range of different Baseline Assessments had some statutory similarities – especially in each child's results being against a measurable scale – but there were also significant differences in style and the scale construction. This made cross-LEA and national comparisons difficult because there was no standard format.

Implications of the introduction of the *Foundation Stage Profile*

The completion of the *Foundation Stage Profile*, in a standard format for all Reception classes, is a statutory requirement. This assessment of every child's attainment measured against all six Areas of Learning has to be undertaken in all schools by the end of the summer term of the Reception year. This is almost a year later than for the original statutory Baseline Assessment. The implications for nursery classes and schools are clear. Under the Baseline Assessment system, children's attainment was assessed early and it gave some real indication of the value that nursery education had added to the child's learning. With assessment now happening at the end of the Reception year, it becomes more difficult to ascertain (and give due credit for) the quality of the work of feeder nurseries. This is true even when the children come from nursery classes in the same school!

Nursery classes and schools need to ensure that they have a clear assessment of children's starting points and to chart their progress throughout their time at the setting. This is not just to ensure that all children make good progress, but also to help practitioners review their own effectiveness as an early years setting. Very often a setting's excellent provision enables young children to encounter vital educational experiences and make rapid headway in their learning. Children who enter good quality settings with low levels of attainment can make major gains in learning because of skilled practitioners' help. The apparent success of a setting, and the hard-won attainment of older children, can sometimes mask the very low attainment that was evident on entry.

Useful tip

You may find the 'Nursery "Value Added"' photocopiable sheet on page 110 helpful.

All nursery settings need to be able to demonstrate the 'value they have added' to their children's learning – in other words, the difference they have made to children's learning and development by what the setting has provided – and this is especially important evidence to present to OFSTED inspectors!

Developing effective entry assessments

It will be important for all nurseries and nursery classes in schools to establish their own entry assessments for the children they serve. However, you do not need a separate system for showing your 'Value Added' – or the positive difference your setting makes to children's education. It can be extrapolated from your normal assessment systems, so long as you have gathered the evidence and undertaken some simple analysis of the overall picture. You can gain the 'Value Added' information by adding a layer of review to your own existing systems!

So how might you gather this information?

➤ Look carefully at the headings you use to gather your current entry information. Do these cover most, or all, six Areas of Learning? Could you extend or adjust these?

➤ Obtain a copy of the new *Foundation Stage Profile* assessment brochure (obtainable from QCA Publications, telephone: 01787 884444).

➤ Look at the sub-divisions for the Areas of Learning for Personal, social and emotional development as they appear in the *Foundation Stage Profile* (Dispositions and attitudes, Social development, Emotional development) and decide whether some of these areas might be usefully incorporated into your entry records. Remember that the statutory assessments are made when children are at the end of their Reception year, so not all the 'boxes' on the scales are likely to be useful to your setting.

➤ Repeat the review for the four sub-divisions of Communication, language and literacy (Language for communication and thinking, Linking sounds and letters, Reading, Writing).

➤ Repeat the task for Mathematical development. (The sub-divisions are: Numbers as labels and for counting, Calculating, Shape, space and measures.)

➤ Add additional sheets to your existing entry assessment to cover any missing areas, for example for Knowledge and understanding of the world.

➤ Over time, as you update your parental discussion records, add extra sections. For example, you might want to find out how confident a child is when visiting new places (KUW) or the range of small and large equipment they use out of the setting (Physical development).

➤ Over time, update any records of discussions with children to add any extra questions or discussion areas you think would be useful to give you a more complete picture.

Collating your overall entry attainment information

Remember, each year group may be different! For each new group of children:

➤ Using a blank copy of your entry assessment record, go through each child's initial assessment. Enter a tick in the Master Copy sections for a positive attainment, leave them blank for a negative

➤ Tally up the positive scores for each section and calculate the percentage (for example, 8/23 pupils = 35% rounded up).

➤   Complete a dated cohort sheet with the overall sections and scores.
➤   In due course, compare this sheet with a similar analysis of children's attainment on leaving. The positive difference will show your 'Value Added'!

Issues for Reception classes

The introduction of the Curriculum Guidance for the Foundation Stage (QCA) was a major step forward in recognising the need for schools to provide an appropriate curriculum for young children. This welcome establishment of a proper Foundation Stage as a phase in its own right has helped school settings have the confidence to provide a special early years curriculum tailored to the needs of their own children. It clarified the educational experiences that best supported learning in the early years. It enabled schools to resist the pressures to introduce a formal and narrow curriculum, engendered by targets, the National Curriculum and league tables. This would have been counter-productive for young children's learning.

Assessment and the *Foundation Stage Profile*

The requirement for all schools to assess children in the first half-term of their entry to school, through Baseline Assessments, gave a sharper focus to assessing young children's development as they joined the Reception classes. Implementing these statutory requirements helped staff be precise in recognising their children's starting-points and in subsequently planning activities and support for their further learning.

The *Foundation Stage Profile* has now superseded the original statutory assessment and has to be completed for each child by the end of the Reception year, although assessments can be made at any time throughout the year, as appropriate for individual children.

This change has major implications for schools, and local education authorities are charged with training staff in the process. LEAs also have the responsibility of appointing appropriately experienced moderators who will follow a programme of individual school visits to moderate assessment processes and standards. They can also organise cluster support to help practitioners become secure in their judgements for assessment.

The *Foundation Stage Profile* scales will be reported to local education authorities for collation and practitioners have some justifiable concerns about the way that this information may be used, fearing additional league tables. However, schools can use the final assessment information themselves to track individual children's progress, to review their early years curriculum to make sure they offer sufficient learning experiences to support all children's learning, and to check the school's 'Value Added' to the end of the Foundation Stage. Make the assessments work for your school setting as valuable evidence for self-review. Schools may retain any personal assessment systems that they already have, and they can use these to record information, but they *must* complete the formal *Foundation Stage Profile*, using the scales for each Area of Learning (including the sub-divisions in Personal, social and emotional development, Communication, language and literacy and Mathematical development) by the end of the summer term in Reception. You are also required to fill in short sections on:

➤ information from previous settings
➤ two parental discussions (one early in the year, one reporting progress and sharing the *Profile* at the end of the year)
➤ discussions with the child.

The next section of this chapter will deal with *Foundation Stage Profile* issues in greater detail.

The Literacy Hour and Numeracy sessions

The National Literacy and Numeracy strategies are not statutory requirements at Reception level, although schools that choose not to follow the respective programmes, need to demonstrate that they follow an equally well-structured curriculum in English and mathematics and that pupils' standards are high enough. However, schools would be well advised to follow the outline of both strategies, as this will ensure that a balanced programme is followed overall.

Reception classes should follow the Foundation Stage curriculum for Communication, language and literacy and Mathematical development overall, but elements of the literacy and numeracy sessions should be built into the programme. Many of the component parts of these strategies, such as 'big book' activities and the modelling of writing or the use of number rhymes, songs and counting games, are in fact drawn from good quality early years practice! In the first two-and-a-half terms of Reception it is better to plan short sessions to cover particular parts of the strategies. These can be built in productively at different times across the day, for instance: a 'big book' activity first with a phonic game much later, or a mathematical shopping game at one time and a sorting and counting activity later in the day.

In the last half of the final term children can generally work up to a full session to prepare them for this approach in Year 1. However, many schools increasingly feel that the transition from the Foundation Stage curriculum to Year 1 is a too radical change for young children. There is increasing evidence that it can work well for Year 1 to continue a Foundation Stage style topic for a few weeks, gradually introducing more formal whole-class literacy and numeracy sessions and other National Curriculum requirements, as the children settle with their new teachers.

OFSTED inspections

Inspectors leading inspections of the Foundation Stage in schools have to be trained and endorsed by OFSTED. Other inspectors will visit and observe the work of the Reception class and contribute their views, but the endorsed inspector will actually write the report section.

Inspectors inspecting Reception classes will look for:

➤ an appropriate curriculum, planned to the *Curriculum Guidance for the Foundation Stage*, with a good balance across all six Areas of Learning
➤ planning and activities that have clear learning objectives linked to the Stepping Stones as well as the Early Learning Goals
➤ lively and imaginative activities which engage children's interest well, with a mix of directed and child-initiated tasks

Useful tip
You may find the 'Reception literacy and numeracy timeline planner' photocopiable sheet on page 111 useful to decide your actions.

➤   staff deployed well to give targeted groups and individuals support and
new challenges
➤   staff assessing on a day-to-day basis and adjusting teaching as necessary
➤   assessment being undertaken systematically, directed towards the
Foundation Stage Profile.

Dealing with the *Foundation Stage Profile*

Throughout the Foundation Stage, as part of good quality
teaching and learning for young children, practitioners will
naturally need to assess every child's development. This
assessment should be the measure of children's individual
progress in relation to the Stepping Stones and Early Learning
Goals – as laid down in the *Curriculum Guidance for the Foundation
Stage.* The assessments will be made by practitioners from making
observations and building a picture of what each child knows,
understands and can do.

The *Foundation Stage Profile* is a summary of practitioners'
assessment knowledge and must be completed by the end of
the Reception year. This replaces the earlier statutory Baseline
Assessment that was undertaken at a child's entry into school.

The Foundation Stage Profile requirements

The *Foundation Stage Profile* sets out the Early Learning Goals in all six Areas
of Learning within a set of 13 assessment scales, each of which contains nine
points (shown as distinct boxes). The areas of Personal, social and emotional
development, Communication, language and literacy and Mathematical
development have been split to give greater precision in assessment detail,
whereas the other areas remain complete. The scales are arranged so that:

➤   the first three points in each section (coloured green) are based mainly on
the Stepping Stones. Characteristically these apply to children at early stages and
are likely to be covered before Early Learning Goals are achieved
➤   the next five points are drawn from the Early Learning Goals themselves
and are laid out in general order of difficulty although, as they are not strictly
hierarchical, some children may achieve these in a different order
➤   the final point of each scale represents a child who is working consistently
beyond the level of the Early Learning Goals
➤   they include an indication of in which term judgements are made.

Practitioners will need to make judgements based on their knowledge of
each child, using a 'best fit' model to determine how to complete the points.
Although practitioners will have sufficient accumulated knowledge to make
assessments in many areas, it is likely that they will need to build in extra
observations in some aspects to make secure judgements. Additionally, earlier
providers, parents/carers and the children themselves are rightly expected
to contribute to the process. Moderators, appointed by local education
authorities, will visit schools and help practitioners become confident in their
final assessments and ensure consistency in judgements. They will also set up
moderation meetings on a rolling programme over time.

Training and support

Local education authorities are required to offer all school settings training in the process. In some areas, other settings can also become involved in training sessions and – where this is available – settings will find such opportunities valuable in considering their own assessment systems and how best to pass on information to schools as their children move on.

Teacher mentors are frequently involved in the programmes and can give you really good guidance and advice. There is also much to be gained by schools working together in cluster groups. This is particularly important so practitioners can come to terms with moderation of what evidence is needed to indicate that a child has securely attained the different points on the scales. However, schools can also share their best practice and ideas for personal assessment approaches. This will help Reception classes refine their own methods.

Key Stage 1 staff tend to be experienced in using 'best fit' assessments, because they have had to make their Teacher Assessments at the end of Key Stage 1. Many Reception staff are already highly-skilled observers but others, new staff or staff new to the age group, will need sensitive support to help them become confident in their judgements.

Positive strategies for success

➤ Ensure that the head teacher allocates time from the school Training Day budget each year for staff to consider the everyday working implications of the new *Profile*, assessment requirements and moderation. (This is essential for school 'Value Added'.)

➤ Review your current assessment and recording system. Decide whether it works well, and make any adjustments that will make it easier to combine with the *Profile*.

➤ Build focused discussions into your parent contact schedule – early in the year and during the last term for *Profile* sharing.

➤ Decide how you will record parents'/carers' views. (The 'Parents' entry contributions' and 'Parents' ongoing contributions' photocopiable sheets on pages 135–136 may be a useful starting-point.)

➤ Where there is a single Reception teacher, ask for the early years coordinator to work alongside – this is not an area that can be covered alone.

➤ Work regularly with clusters, or take the initiative and approach neighbouring schools to look at a range of different evidence together. This could take place over tea and cakes for a relaxed social dimension!

➤ Set up occasional, short, joint observations to build confidence and consistency. Ask the head teacher for some cover time, perhaps during assembly or at another suitable time.

➤ Set up staff INSET on observation techniques. (You may find the 'Observation techniques' photocopiable sheet on page 140 helpful as a focus.)

➤ Use your teacher mentor or moderators! They are there to offer you support and can give you ideas from good practice.

➤ Build in a block of time every month, at designated planning meetings, for review. Check on observations and how much information staff are collecting on individuals. Decide if secure assessments can be pencilled into a child's *Profile*.

➤ Set up termly reviews to ensure that every child is being observed, and correct any missing elements. Complete all secure *Profile* sections for the term.

➤ Look at your planning and build in extra observations within your normal programme, with named personnel, to supplement your knowledge base.

➤   Build in a termly rolling programme of individual discussions with children. (The 'Child's record sheet – early days' and the 'Child's record sheet – ongoing' photocopiable sheets on pages 137–138 may be useful.)

Assessment and issues for other settings

Although non-school settings may not have the statutory requirements for assessment that apply to Reception classes, there is still an expectation that they will take assessment seriously. This does not mean that every setting needs to have a highly formalised assessment system in place. It does mean that settings need to observe all their children carefully and make professional judgements about their development, and then use this information to plan the best way to help them make further progress.

   Those settings that seek funding for their provision have to demonstrate that they provide an educational programme that follows the *Curriculum Guidance for the Foundation Stage*. This means that their provision must cover the six Areas of Learning in a balanced manner and that the children will have opportunities to a full range of educational experiences, which will enable them to progress through the Stepping Stones and towards the Early Learning Goals.

Assessment is important in all settings, because:

➤   practitioners need to know the starting-points for learning for each child in order to plan the next steps

➤   settings need to know the unique learning needs of the community they serve, so that an appropriate overall programme can be planned

➤   practitioners need to involve parents/carers in the assessment process, so that they can support their children's learning more effectively at home

➤   settings are able to identify children with special educational needs early on and can help them make good progress through swift and well-focused intervention or by alerting other agencies

➤   settings can provide strong evidence, based on a good knowledge of each child, to pass on to schools and other settings to aid a smooth transition and help new staff build on children's learning and interests

➤   schools and other settings may request records of any assessment information a feeder setting holds

➤   OFSTED inspectors will expect to have evidence that positive approaches to assessment are used.

Skilled observation is the key to accurate assessment

Early years practitioners are usually skilled informal assessors. Their everyday work and contact with children enables them to observe many different activities and the manner in which children react to them. Most practitioners will easily acquire an informal bank of knowledge about the children they work with. They can generally recall a series of pictures in their minds of specific children engaged in a range of tasks and learning experiences. They will often share with colleagues and parents the differences between a child's early days at the setting and how they present at a later date. In many settings, ongoing discussions with parents and carers are the norm, happening almost on a daily basis, as children arrive or are collected! In most settings there will be a variety of staff and helpers who have contact with the children. They may all have opportunities to see children at work and play, and have valuable information to contribute to the assessment process. However, observation is a skilled process and everyone needs to focus carefully to glean the most useful information.

Developing observation skills

Most settings will have staff and helpers with very different levels of experience and training. For some, observation has been a key area in the past, for others (particularly helpers) this may be a less developed skill. Staff may be actively involved in supporting groups rather than noting specific children's responses. It is very difficult to be directly teaching a group of children and observing every individual's precise reactions. (Chapters 4 and 6 deal with this in more detail.)

Planning and assessment

Your setting's planning will cover the range of different activities that you offer to children at different times. In Chapter 1 you will find guidance on how planning can be undertaken. It is important to identify a manageable number of activities each week where specific children can be observed by a nominated member of staff. (For further guidance, please refer to the first section of this chapter 'Linking assessment opportunities into your curriculum'.)

OFSTED inspections

All personnel engaged in inspecting settings will have had relevant OFSTED training, and will have been assessed. They will generally spend only one day in your setting and are unlikely to see first-hand everything in your provision. However, they will want to report on the main aspects of your provision and your work with parents. It is sensible to gather together as much evidence as you can and keep this in preparation for your next OFSTED inspection visit. You may find the 'OFSTED inspection checklist' photocopiable sheet on page 112 useful.

Inspectors will want to see that:

➤ your curriculum is planned following the *Curriculum Guidance for the Foundation Stage* (QCA), and all six Areas of Learning are covered
➤ you use both the Stepping Stones and the Early Learning Goals as part of your planning
➤   there are lively and imaginative activities which excite children's interest
➤ there is a good balance of directed and child-initiated tasks and play
➤ adults interact sensitively with children and extend their learning
➤ children of different ages are presented with a variety of work which challenges them appropriately
➤ children of different abilities and developmental stages have appropriate levels of support
➤ staff and helpers are deployed to give targeted groups or individuals support
➤ staff assess on a daily basis and adjust their teaching approach as necessary
➤ you have in place a good induction programme with parents being made to feel welcome
➤ you are implementing a manageable and structured assessment and record-keeping system.

Chapter 3 Manageable assessment systems

> ➤ **Creating a useful system**
> ➤ **Entry assessment**
> ➤ **Setting up the system – timescales and personnel issues**
> ➤ **Creating the system in the six Areas of Learning**

Creating a useful system

The assessment system you already use may be perfectly adequate. Assessment systems do not have to be bulky and elaborate.

They need to:

➤ work for your setting (with the staff and time you have available)
➤ be of a manageable size, so that vast amounts of paperwork and time are not involved
➤ be user-friendly and easy to maintain
➤ focus firmly on children's learning and development
➤ easily give staff, parents/carers and children a clear picture of progress
➤ be helpful for new staff joining your setting
➤ be useful to show evidence of learning and progress at times to other agencies, inspectors and so on
➤ be useful to inform receiving schools and other settings.

You might find it helpful to refer to the 'System review' photocopiable sheet on page 113 to check whether your current arrangements are fine as they are or whether any adjustments will make them even more useful. Share the sheet with your staff and check through the sections together.

If you feel some adjustments are necessary, consult your teacher mentor and other nearby settings and ask to share examples of assessment systems. Arrange a visit or invite colleagues over to you and look at each other's systems. You may find that you have much to offer your colleagues and between you build up a bank of very practical ideas. Also consider the following examples of how different settings have approached the issue.

After you have investigated a few systems, review your own arrangements and get everyone to make suggestions for improvement. Decide on the best ideas and then set a deadline for introducing a new system at the beginning of the next admission time.

Example 1 – Sunnyside Playgroup

The group meets for five 2½-hour morning sessions only, in a local Guides'
Hall. It serves a wide area with children coming from many varied social and
economic backgrounds. There is a mix of three- and four-year-olds, with a total
of 24 children. There are three staff, supported by two helpers for most sessions
and many parents/carers stay.

➤ An allocated 'link' member of staff spends about 20 minutes with each
parent/carer on entry, completing a simple questionnaire regarding the child's
likes/dislikes, general development, personality, plus emergency contacts and
health issues. They informally observe the child together and talk about the
activities on offer.

➤ An A4 envelope file is started for each child, containing sheets headed
with the six Areas of Learning. Staff review each child's progress and major
developments at a half-termly lunch meeting, with all staff contributing. The
'link' practitioner updates the file and arranges to meet the parent (for about 15
minutes) to discuss this and share ways to support learning at home. Parents'/
carers' comments are added.

➤ Due to shared accommodation, no records can be left. The leader safeguards
the files. Samples of children's paintings and emergent writing are added.

➤ The files are sent on to the feeder schools or other settings in due course.

Example 2 – Treetops Nursery

This private nursery caters for around 30 children, all three- and four-year-olds,
in a city centre setting. There are two main sessions a day (each of 3 hours
duration), but about ten children stay all day. There is a teacher plus four nursery
nurses. A few parents/carers help occasionally, but this is relatively rare.

➤ Parents/primary carers complete a standard entry questionnaire (child's
preferences, health, development, past experience and so on) with the teacher,
who begins a clip file.

➤ Staff observe, take photographs of new children's activities and report to the
teacher, who meets the parents/carers again later to discuss how child is settling
in and what progress they are making.

➤ At weekly team meetings, staff report significant observations and give
samples of children's work to the teacher who updates the file. The team
discusses activities and approaches to be planned for the child during the next
few weeks.

➤ The teacher sees parents/carers on a termly basis to report progress in all six
Areas of Learning and to share ideas for home support.

➤ The setting completes personal record sheets, which match the scales and
points of the *Foundation Stage Profile*, with extra sheets for work samples and
for comments.

➤ These are given to parents/carers when their child moves on to school or
another setting.

Example 3 – High Street Primary School (nursery and Reception classes)

The school serves a mixed area. The nursery caters for 60 pupils, all part-time, giving priority to the oldest children. Most children attend the nursery before Reception class. Many children come from families where English is not spoken at home.

➤ The nursery closes for several days during the year to enable staff to make paired home visits to new parents/carers. (Nursery nurses sometimes use part of their Training Days.) Where necessary, bilingual staff or volunteer interpreters from the community help parents/carers complete a standard entry information sheet.

➤ Before entry, children and parents are invited – a few at a time – to join part of a session. The children's group leader is freed up to greet the child, talk to the parents/carers, and take a photograph to go on the front of the child's named 'Personal book'. The leader shows them this (a ring-binder file) and explains that this will be completed all through the Foundation Stage to show the child's progress.

➤ Staff make targeted observations of newcomers for the first three weeks. A meeting is held to record significant points on a dedicated 'starting-points' sheet, under Areas of Learning headings, and to plan specific activities, adapted from the existing planned programmes, for these children.

➤ Discussions on progress and ways to support children at home are held with new parents/carers within the first half-term, and termly thereafter.

➤ The 'Personal book' has pages relating to the *Foundation Stage Profile* scales and points, which are updated each half-term. It includes photographs, samples of work, notes and Post-its. It goes with the child to Reception.

➤ In Reception classes, two children are targeted each day for special observation. Some specific 15-minute observations are set up (for example, outdoor play and group activities) with an allocated staff member. Results are entered in the 'Personal book' at the end of each day. Staff then plan activities to match children's emerging needs.

➤ The 'Personal Book' feeds into the Profile, which is completed in the summer term. A simplified copy of this forms the basis of the report to parents/carers and is passed to Year 1.

Entry assessment

Whatever your type of setting, you will want to gather information about children's backgrounds, previous experience, health issues and general likes, dislikes and interests. All this information will help you to know each child better and will help you plan appropriate activities, which are likely to enable them to settle happily. It will also give you some idea of the starting-points for each child.

Background information

It will be important for you to begin to build positive relationships with each child's parents or carers, so that they feel confident in leaving their child with you and they are happy to approach you with any worries or concerns that may arise. It is important too for the child to feel secure and valued in your setting, so that they can settle in swiftly and become familiar with routines and arrangements. Simple things, such as knowing, and using, a child's siblings' names, will help a child feel safe and welcome. It is obviously also very important to know the parent or carer you will have most to do with and to explain how discussions on their child's progress will be shared.

Previous experience

You will need to know what, if any, previous setting experience each child had had. For example, a child who has been to a playgroup setting before joining you, may well have become used to playing alongside others and sharing resources. An only child, with no previous early years setting experience, is less likely to have had similar social interaction.

Where a child has attended a previous setting, you should obtain details from the parents/carers. Try to contact the leader or manager and ask for any assessment information they can forward to you. Also ask the parents/carers themselves, as many settings pass simple records (children's work and notes on progress) on to them. If such records are available, you can include these with your own entry assessment materials, or you can make a brief summary of what the child has had experience of, knows, understands and can do, and use this as part of your own starting record.

Reception classes must complete the *Foundation Stage Profile* by the end of the summer term, and they are expected to use assessment information from previous settings wherever possible. The very first section on the *Profile* relates to this under the box title 'Information about the child from previous settings'. Any information should give you valuable insight into previous learning and experience. However, remember that children may react and respond differently in quite different circumstances and you will need to make an early assessment of each child within your own setting.

Health issues

This can be a sensitive area, but it is vital that you have relevant information in order to safeguard each child. This information is best collected at a face-to-face discussion with parents/carers when you can adopt a warm and reassuring stance. If you undertake home visits, this is an ideal opportunity to collect this type of information in an environment where the parent feels at ease. A worried parent of an asthmatic child will not necessarily know that your setting has other young sufferers and that you are confident in your caring arrangements. If home visits are not part of your induction programme, set aside time for a brief discussion with each parent or carer. To maximise the limited time available, some settings send out questionnaires before such a meeting and then discuss these privately with the parents/carers in due course. It will be particularly important to record any allergies that the child may have and any immediate action that must be taken if there are problems.

However, there may be other health-related conditions that parents/carers raise with you that are new for your setting. In such cases, you should ask the parent to supply as much formal information for you as possible and, importantly, give you a health worker contact, which you can follow up to

Useful tip

If parents/carers enlist family members or childminders to bring their child to the setting, it may be necessary to make special, agreed arrangements for primary carers to be involved in any discussions.

discuss caring and learning implications before the child is admitted. In extreme cases, the child may have been identified as having special educational needs and may be entitled to specialist support. It is advisable to clip copies of all relevant health information, including written comments by the parents/carers, to your initial assessment records.

   Although most information should stay in a child's file, health issues need special attention. A composite sheet containing the most vital health information collated from all the new children's entry assessments should be compiled and shared with your setting's staff, so all are alerted to possible problems and know what to do.

Children's preferences and interests

Each child is unique and will already have formed early preferences and interests. Some of these are likely to change over time, others will not! At the simplest level these may be related to food choices, which will be vital for you to know for snack time and cookery sessions. However, information about children's interests will be valuable in helping you organise activities and give you opportunities to extend children's learning. For example, a child who confidently uses a computer at home can probably work at a more demanding level in your setting. A child who has a passionate interest in dinosaurs can be drawn into reading dinosaur-based books. Conversely, knowing that a child is very timid about boisterous activities, or dislikes animals, can help you plan ways to support them individually and so help them overcome their nervousness.

Useful tip
Each setting needs to develop a personalised entry assessment to determine each child's starting-point. You may find the 'Early days assessment' photocopiable sheet on page 114 useful to help you set up the very first elements of your setting's assessment system.

Setting up the system – timescales and personnel issues

An effective assessment system cannot be created overnight! The best systems tend to evolve over time, with staff making adjustments in the light of experience. Your system has to be tailored to the constraints of your staffing and time available. However, all settings are expected to have an assessment system in place and, importantly, to use the information gleaned to help children learn.

Inspection issues

OFSTED inspections of early years settings report many good quality examples, but frequently criticise the limitations of assessment. Even in settings where assessment programmes have been put in place, inspectors sometimes find that, although useful information is recorded adequately, staff do not always use this enough. Opportunities to call together children at the same stage of development for special activities, to challenge individual children ready for further learning, or to give children real chances to work through their own ideas and interests are often missed.

Inspectors also often identify the need for more attention to ensure that precise observations are made of children's role-play, outdoor play and free-choice activities. These are areas where children are frequently given only limited supervision, because other groups are engaged in tasks that demand a heavy input of adult intervention. However, these activities can give practitioners a real insight into children's knowledge and understanding in many of the six Areas of Learning.

Making a start

In Chapter 2, the important features of an assessment cycle were covered, based on six key steps:

➤ gathering previous information
➤ first parent/carer contact
➤ first admission
➤ after settling
➤ regular, timed progress checks
➤ summative assessment.

These form the key marker posts of a manageable system. It will be useful to carry out 'Our assessment cycle planner' photocopiable sheet on page 109 with all staff, before finalising any new or adapted system in your setting. This will help you list any elements that need further discussion.

Practical suggestions and considerations

➤ Begin to compile a list of addresses and contacts at previous settings commonly attended by your children. Add brief notes to cover the type of provision, number of sessions, the usual time spent there, as well as any specific points, such as 'Steiner provision' or other links. This should save time, make enquiries easier and help all staff have a clear picture of a child's past experience.
➤ Try to build up relationships with feeder settings where possible. Send them a brief outline of your provision (a brochure or newsletter, for example) and

let them know that children often join your setting. To share the load, nominate a named member of your staff to take responsibility as 'link' for each feeder setting.
➤ Build up contacts and keep an accessible record of named personnel and addresses in a similar way for other agencies (health, specialist services, social services and so on), so that these can be contacted as necessary. Add each new contact to the list as these arise.
➤ If appropriate, consider asking a named member of your staff to act as 'liaison link' to take a lead in multi-agency work. This might be the staff member with responsibility for special educational needs (or SENCO), but other staff can share the workload and broaden their professional experience.
➤ Decide whether or not home visits are appropriate for your setting. In some areas parents/carers are available and appreciate the opportunity to discuss their child in their own homes, and staff can see the child in familiar surroundings. In other areas, generally with a high proportion of working parents, this is less effective.

 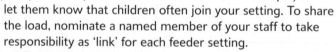

➤ If home visits are to be planned, these should only be undertaken in pairs. This is for personal safety reasons, and also allows one member of staff to talk to the parents/carers and possibly complete admission information, whilst the other can get to know the child.

➤ If visits are to be organised, work out how this can be practically arranged. For all settings, apart from Reception classes, you might allocate a few days each year when your setting is closed to follow a timetable of visits. In Reception classes, the head teacher might permit non-teaching staff to use some of their INSET time.

➤ Allow all new children a settling-in period of at least two weeks before you make firm initial assessments. Work out a rolling programme of observations by named personnel. To confirm findings, ensure that more than one observation is made. It will be useful if new children are targeted for special note by all staff and that a meeting is held where all can contribute their observations. The 'Early days assessment' photocopiable sheet on page 114 might be helpful for staff use.

➤ Timetable dates for the new children's parental interviews and send details home in good time so that parents/carers can make arrangements. Hold these at a convenient time after your sessions, using a rolling programme over several days. Nominate a staff member to talk to parents/carers and another (if possible) to supervise waiting children and siblings. Organise some games to keep the children happily occupied. Use the opportunity to prepare attractively presented 'Home ideas' packs, or 'How to help your child' suggestion cards, with activities tailored for specific children and share these with parents/carers.

➤ Timetable short observations of target children each week, by named staff to report back and record findings. (Include play and free-choice observations.)

➤ Timetable dates for ongoing parental interviews throughout the rest of the year. The timings will depend on your setting's circumstances. Some settings will wish to repeat the rolling programme of meetings on a termly basis, and this will be particularly useful in keeping parents/carers informed of their children's progress, with time to involve them in supporting their children's learning. Other settings might opt for a different timetable and a more informal approach. However, opportunities for parental contact with dedicated time to discuss children's progress need to be regular and must not be left to chance.

➤ Additionally, Reception classes will need to plan a summer-term session to fit in with their school's overall parental consultation schedules. It is advisable to periodically discuss the *Foundation Stage Profile* and their children's progress with parents/carers throughout the year, as this will form the basis of reports to parents/carers at the end of the Reception class and they should then be familiar with it.

Creating the system in the six Areas of Learning

In order to give the broadest assessment coverage for your children and the most useful information for planning your programmes, it is important to ensure that your system fully addresses all six Areas of Learning. It is sensible to look at the way that children will be ultimately assessed at the end of the Foundation Stage, using the *Foundation Stage Profile* at the end of the Reception class, and to consider how your assessment can dovetail with this.

If your setting caters for younger children, the assessment points (or boxes) of the *Profile* are still a useful framework as these are based firmly on the Stepping Stones and the Early Learning Goals. However, you will not need to be concerned about calculating assessment scales and reporting these to your local education authority in the way Reception classes in schools must! If you are a nursery attached to a school, or feeding into a school, the use of a simplified *Profile* will make passing on your assessments much easier to match into the Reception-class assessment requirements. This will make transition smoother for your children – as well as building good relationships with your colleagues.

The *Foundation Stage Profile* is set out in a useful way, with each element of the six Areas broken down into sections, with greater sub-divisions for Personal, social and emotional development, Communication, language and literacy and Mathematical development, to aid precise assessment. Each section has a row of green assessment boxes (generally for younger children), grey boxes (generally for the average child in the Foundation Stage) and pink boxes (for those children consistently operating beyond the Early Learning Goals). This means that you can focus predominantly on the rows that best match your intake, although all settings could have children who operate at different levels, or (because the grey row is not hierarchical) in some aspects of the different levels.

Building up a complementary assessment system

The 'Six Areas of Learning – assessment focus sheet' photocopiable sheets on pages 115–127 are designed to unpack the *Foundation Stage Profile* points and boxes. Each one has been laid out to show where the Profile's composite rows are marked. You can best profit from these by:

➤ using them as a basis for staff training – over time – to help familiarise everyone with the different components. Get all staff to look together at each sheet in turn. Ask them to decide which sections apply most to your children. Then discuss the kind of evidence they would need to observe to know that children had attained the different elements
➤ photocopying them for each child in your setting and including them in each child's assessment book or file, ready for completion in due course. You can even colour the sections green, grey and pink!
➤ enlarging each sheet, or selected sheets, and pinning these up in a staff room. Add an assessment 'target child's' name to the top. Ask everyone to observe any significant evidence and write this on dated, detailed Post-it Notes and attach them to each sheet. Fill any secure judgements in the 'Attained' section. Transfer the sheets to the child's file. Note any learning needs and build these into planning
➤ enlarging sheets and laminating them. Display for general use as above. Fill these in with a dry-board marker and Post-it Notes. Transfer all information to a smaller copy in the child's file and reuse the laminated sheet
➤ using the sheets as a basis for discussions with parents/carers about how their children are progressing.

Chapter 4 Productive day-to-day assessment

> ➤ **Using assessment to build in further learning**
> ➤ **Targetting individuals and groups**
> ➤ **Assessing undirected free-choice activities**
> ➤ **Assessing outdoor activities and home- or other play-area sessions**
> ➤ **Involving children in assessment**
> ➤ **The most effective use of staff**

Using assessment to build in further learning

The most important purpose of assessment is to recognise each child's stage of development, so that activities and experiences can be planned to extend learning appropriately. The most elaborate assessment system in the world will be of little value unless practitioners use the information it reveals to help plan further programmes that enable each child to learn, building on what they know, understand and can do already.

Most practitioners already gather much informal information from their day-to-day interactions with their children. The most effective staff can almost intuitively adjust their approaches to children based on what they observe or the reactions they note.

Skilful and positive interaction with children

Observation is the key to successful assessment and practitioners have excellent opportunities to do this, watching children at play or working together. The skill is to know when to stand back and when to move learning on.

You need to stand back and let the activity run unhindered when children are deeply involved in their role-play. Watch the interactions between the group and be ready to gently challenge the children to think hard within their context. In all activities, one of the best ways to encourage learning is through skilful, open-ended questioning techniques.

After any activity, reflect on what you have witnessed and consider how you can build further learning into your programme. This might mean an adjustment by selecting a group of children at the same level for a special activity or by staff directing them to a task designed to build on previous learning or perceived needs. The following examples illustrate this well.

Example 1 – Home-play activity: free choice (Reception class)

A practitioner is informally observing a group of three children in the home-play area. She watches a boy preparing a meal. He has put on an apron and insists the other two do the same. As he works the boy gives instructions to the others to bring him a range of exotic ingredients: 'Lemon grass, fish sauce, Thai rice, please'. Although they are not sure what these are, the two children produce plastic fruit and containers, presenting them to him and repeating the names aloud. He also tells them how he wants the table laid: 'With mats because the curry bowl will be hot' and, 'Napkins and spoons'. The other children are not sure what napkins are and the boy explains, but there are none available in the home-area resources. The practitioner suggests making some from paper and two girls go off to select some large sheets of sugar paper and scissors.

While they are away, the practitioner engages with the boy and asks, 'What are you cooking today?' The boy replies, 'Green Thai curry,' and he continues stirring a wok. She probes further, 'Who's coming to dinner?' to which the boy replies, 'Lots of people are coming to our restaurant tonight. I'm the chef!' The practitioner is surprised he knows the term 'chef' and continues, 'Well chef, I'm a new waitress, can you tell me what to do?' The boy insists that she wears an apron and gets a pad and pencil to take the orders, so he knows how much to cook. He is very knowledgeable and articulate. He explains, 'My uncle's a chef, just like me!'.

Soon the girls return and begin to cut and fold napkins, but they make these far too small. One of them thinks there should be a menu and the chef asks the 'waitress' to help them make it, explaining that it should say 'Green Thai curry'. The practitioner asks the boy to suggest initial letter sounds for this and he identifies 'g', 't' and 'c', saying, 'I've seen them at the restaurant.' The practitioner encourages two children to come to the restaurant and they are served a meal.

After the activity, the practitioner discusses the event with the nursery nurse. They decide to extend the boy's learning, by asking him to create a restaurant area and getting him to write labels, make signs and job lists. They decide that the girls would benefit from making improved menus and looking at real napkins and table mats to try to match size and shape in their own creations. They decide that they will have this as a group-directed activity the next day.

Example 2 – Outdoor play: gardening activity (nursery group)

The children had each planted sunflower seeds in pots and watched them grow on the window sill. The practitioner explains that these now need planting in the garden and tells the children that they will all be gardeners today. They all go outside and she asks everyone to suggest a place, encouraging the older children to give reasons for their choice. After discussion, an area is chosen and the practitioner then chooses two less physically confident children to use spades to dig and prepare a patch of soil. A more coordinated child is asked to demonstrate and help them. When the soil is loosely dug over, children take turns to rake it smooth. The practitioner then asks, 'How shall we plant our flowers?' The children decide they want rows. She pushes further, 'How can we keep our rows straight?' One child suggests marking lines on the soil, but another says, 'We won't see them when we plant our sunflowers, we'll tread on them.' Another suggests placing skipping ropes along the soil, which is agreed and carried out.

The practitioner asks who had seen people 'planting out'. A girl says, 'I helped my mummy. We bought the plants and put them in the garden.' The practitioner asks her to show everyone what she did. She demonstrates (with help) and then the children take turns to plant their sunflowers, choosing a spot. Whilst they wait, the practitioner asks how they will know which plant is theirs and they suggest using labels. Felt-tipped pens, lolly sticks and luggage tags are produced for the children's choice. The more advanced children are directed to write their own names unaided, and the practitioner helps the less confident children. After planting and labelling, everyone helps water the plants.

After reflection, the practitioner helps the more able to draw up a plan of their planting. She challenges most children to write their names on sticky labels to attach, supporting only a few. An 'Our garden' book is made, with each child directed, as appropriate to their level, to draw, use diagrams or 'write' about their gardening work.

Targetting individuals and groups

The results of observations are most constructively employed in the planning of how best to meet the needs of individuals and groups. In the last section there were two examples of how staff in different settings observed group activities and noted the various stages of children engaged in the tasks. After due reflection, further activities were planned to extend the learning of children according to their stage of development. Therefore, in one observation, a boy who was observed operating at a high level in some aspects of Communication, language and literacy, was later guided towards developing his writing to build on his current knowledge. However, in the same observation, two girls were noted as needing more opportunities to develop their awareness of relative size and shape within overall Mathematical development, as well as some areas of Communication, language and literacy. In this instance, the practitioner decided that a directed group task would be of greatest benefit to the children. Having made a number of observations in different curriculum areas, she acted upon them and followed up the initial task.

Useful tip
Use the 'Planning for learning' photocopiable sheet on page 128. Share it with staff, who were not involved in the observation, but are organising further activities. It also provides a good agenda when consulting with others on the best way forward.

The importance of reflection

During some observations, staff will automatically think of wonderfully exciting ways to develop children's learning further! However, in most busy settings, there may be limited time to do anything about it immediately, because staff will need to move on to their next supervision.

If it is possible, when you are allocating time for observations, try to plan for the actual observation, plus about 10–15 minutes reflection afterwards. Ideally, this should be somewhere quiet, away from the demands and hubbub of a setting's activity. In this quiet period, think through ideas for how you can plan the next steps in learning from what you have just seen, taking notes if you deem it necessary.

Use the time to consider the most important issues for each child's development. You may have identified a number of Areas of Learning, which would benefit from attention, but bear in mind that it is not possible to address everything at once! Reflect on which are the most immediate and important areas for further learning. By all means, note all areas, but concentrate on those where you can make the greatest difference. Do not overlook the more advanced children, however, as they are also entitled to make progress at their own level.

Consulting other colleagues

The information that you glean from observations will be extremely important. It can tell you things about children's needs and their progress that may not have been known before. Busy practitioners need to share information together to maximise the valuable time allocated to direct observation and to share expertise and knowledge.

After observation and reflection, feedback briefly to colleagues and discuss together how children's needs could be met.

➤ Decide whether any further observations are needed to corroborate your judgements. If so, who will carry these out and when?
➤ Feedback particular individual priority needs.
➤ Identify children who have possible group needs.
➤ Share any ideas for tasks and activities that would be beneficial.
➤ Ask colleagues for ideas on how to help meet the identified children's needs.
➤ Consider your setting's weekly planned programme and decide whether there are planned activities that would adequately meet the developmental needs of these children.
➤ Plan how best to include identified children in these activities:
  • Could an able child occasionally join a group working at a higher level?
  • Could groups be extended to include extra children with the same developmental needs?
  • Could a member of staff focus on individuals/groups within the programme?
  • Could a directed activity, related to your planned programme, be set up for an individual or group?
  • Could a helper step in to support or challenge specific children?
➤ Identify learning needs that cannot be met through your current programme.
➤ Decide how these can be met:
  • Is there an activity planned in the near future that will meet the needs that have been identified?
  • Will an activity need to be set up? How will it be done and who will do it?

● Are there ways to involve parents/carers to support further learning at home?

● Are there special needs issues identified that require further action? Can other agencies offer support?

● Are the needs of children whose mother tongue is not English, an issue? Can the help of other agencies be sought?

➤ Finalise what action will be taken and how the identified children's progress will be reviewed.

Targetting individuals

Many settings carry out a rolling programme of individual observations to ensure that all children are observed over time. Each session one or two children are identified for staff special focus. Sometimes this ties in with a child's 'Special Day' when they have their turn to help with certain jobs (for example, serving snacks, leading children outside, or making choices). If a child is away, they are not put at the bottom of the list, but are put on a 'holding system' to be fitted in as soon as possible.

The flexibility of a rolling programme means it is possible to include some children (for example, those with special educational needs or where staff have concerns) more frequently than others. Children's names can be displayed for staff, or an enlarged session list of names can have two red arrows that are moved to indicate target children.

Observations may then be made by named staff, who are 'off duty' elsewhere in the setting, or by all staff. 'Dedicated observers' may follow the target child from activity to activity or observe for a set time, according to the constraints of the setting. Staff are asked to take note of any significant achievements or concerns. For children being reassessed, specific information can be requested, such as how well a child uses phonic knowledge to write. Due note should be made of how much progress has been made since the previous assessment. (The 'Planning for learning' photocopiable sheet on page 128 can be used). After the session all staff feed back briefly, giving a broad picture of how each child functioned in different situations. This is then recorded in the child's file.

In some settings, children are involved in the process and staff hold short discussions with them. (This is dealt with in more detail later in this chapter).

Targetting groups

In some settings it is more manageable to target groups of children for observation and assessment. In an average setting with 30 children per session, it might only take one week with carefully selected groups to observe all the children. Where there is limited staff availability, this may be useful, and some settings earmark one week each half-term for this process. Alternatively, group observations may be a constructive method of covering specific aspects of the six Areas of Learning, or to get a general overview of children's needs to help you plan further work. In effective settings, a combination of group and individual observations and assessment will be the order of the day.

To maximise group observations, the target children should work together in a fairly compact area. It is too difficult, and wastes valuable time, to try to keep track of children who move to work in different places around your setting! Ideally, all the children should be engaged in a related task, working together in a group of no more than six. To observe a group fully, it is desirable for the observer not to be involved in any teaching or direct supervision. If this is impossible, try to work with even smaller groups.

Useful tip

The 'Target group' photocopiable sheet' on page 129 is designed to help you manage this process.

Special needs issues

In every setting, there are likely to be children with special educational needs of some sort. All settings have a responsibility to help children with SEN learn as well as they can and should have a SENCO to oversee SEN issues. You may be aware of some children through contact with parents/carers, other settings or other agencies, such as the health service or pre-school special needs support services. In these cases, you should have some useful information about the children's needs and any available support, but it will be vital to track their progress over time and also to consider how you can adapt your approach to help them learn best. In other cases, it will be children's general presentation and your observations that alert you to their possible special educational needs.

Settings need to arrange an Annual Review, with discussions with parents/carers and relevant agencies, for any children that are identified as having SEN within your setting. In readiness for this you will need to keep precise records of your provision for them and also their responses and progress. Children with SEN will require you to draw up Individual Education Plans (IEPs) to pinpoint learning needs and targets and how you will address these. These must be referred to at Reviews, overseen by the SENCO, shared with all staff and updated regularly. To check children's progress and determine particular learning difficulties, you will have to make very careful observations.

You will need to observe children with SEN within general groups, so that you have information about how they cope in different circumstances, but also in small supported groups and individually. You will also need to draw upon the widest staff observations – with very specific examples – not just for your records and to track progress towards targets, but also to share practical strategies that help children learn the most effectively. Detailed observations, with evidence of work, will be essential to gain extra support for any child who you feel needs Early Years Action Plus. Genuine attempts to gain extra support from specialist services have often been delayed through lack of precise evidence and information.

Children with English as an additional language

Careful observation will enable your setting not to confuse special educational needs with a lack of progress because of a child's limited acquisition of English. Fluency will improve with time and good teaching! Become aware of any multicultural support services that exist in your area and familiarise yourself with the resources and specialist advice available. Ask whether there is any bilingual support for children and also for discussions with parents/carers, especially for completing pre-entry information and for reporting progress.

Many LEAs can arrange the translation of forms into mother tongues, but be aware that many minority ethnic families may prefer to have the help of bilingual volunteers in initial discussions, completing paperwork and when meeting staff. Seek out local community leaders (the local library can often help with contacts) and ask for their advice. Often they will organise volunteer translators for you.

Assessing undirected free-choice activities

In any good setting there will be opportunities during the day for the children to decide the activities they wish to follow. Careful observation will reveal much about children's personal interests and experience and this will help practitioners plan future work that will irresistibly capture the children's imagination! The following example illustrates that even when children branch out from the intended course, observation can still be extremely valuable.

Camping in the greenhouse!

A practitioner was unobtrusively observing a group of five nursery children as they played with some small-world equipment, including some model greenhouses which had been included on purpose. (The staff were developing some work within the local area and were planning a garden-centre visit.)

The children, who were not familiar with the idea of greenhouses, decided to use them as tents! This prompted much discussion on camping and resulted in the group arranging the greenhouses into rows, following the lead of a child who talked about camping with her family. Another child had visited his older brother at a Cub camp and explained that the tents could be arranged round a campfire. The children rearranged the layout and then began to talk about camping. They decided that they wanted to build their own tent and campsite.

They went off to find materials to help, and found wooden bricks and newspaper, fabric lengths in the dressing-up box, and plates and beakers from the home-play area. Using several chairs, they draped the fabric to make the tent, but this kept sliding off. After disagreeing about how to solve the problem, they decided to split up and build two tents facing each other. The observer watched and listened to each pair in turn, making notes on the agreed sheet, under all Areas of Learning.

One pair asked the observer for scissors and string, but she quietly directed them to a helper, who provided the materials and, under the children's direction, helped them tie the fabric. The other pair worked unaided, using clothes pegs to fasten the tent. A younger child quietly arranged the bricks and newspaper to make a campfire. With immense delight the children crowded into the tents to see if they were big enough. They selected dressing-up clothes to make sleeping bags, cooked their supper, ate it and went to bed! The observer later completed the sheet, focusing on Personal, social and emotional development, Communication, language and literacy, and Creative development, but with some references to Mathematical development (shape, space and measures), Physical development and Knowledge and understanding of the world.

Capturing the information

The keys to success in this example are:

➤ the practitioner is unobtrusively observing and not disturbing the flow of the play activity, even though it is taking an unexpected route
➤ although children appeal to her for help, she redirects them to another helper who knows that an observation is underway and fills the support gap
➤ children are obviously used to having adults quietly observing them and accept her redirection easily

➤ the observer divides her time between the children as they work – she is realistic about what can be achieved in the time
➤ she uses an agreed format to record her observations
➤ the form is completed later, after reflection and reference to the Foundation Stage curriculum.

Refer to the 'Undirected-play observation' photocopiable sheet on page 130 for a format that can be used successfully to capture the assessment information. The practitioner observing the group used this format to record the most significant evidence from the session, as you can see from the completed section reproduced below.

Productive day-to-day assessment (Chapter 4)

Undirected-play observation

Complete a record in columns 1 and 2, then reflect and complete column 3

General activity:- Small-world activity - introduction of greenhouse models - free play session, no direction.   **Date:** 23rd June **Time:** 2 - 2.30pm

Participating children (* star those targeted)	What happened (content, participation, choices, perseverance, cooperation, collaboration, problem-solving, communication, use of knowledge, skills, individual's contribution)		Related Areas of Learning (to be completed later)
Josh *	Children played with greenhouses but didn't know what they were - decided they could be tents!	Took the lead, showing children how tents are arranged on campsites. Spoke about his family experiences. Selected chairs for tent supports and led discussions on fixing fabric. Worked with Sunil to make tent; suggested using pegs.	PSE (DA) 3,5,6,7,8,9 PD 3,5 CLL (LCT) 5,6,7,8 CD 7,8
Sunhil		Was keen to build own camp, suggested Cub model having listened to others' ideas. Worked with Josh, under his direction, but persevered with tricky pegging. Suggested making sleeping bags.	PSE (DA) 3,5,6 PD 3,5 CLL(LCT) 5,6,7,8 CD 3,7,8
Hyacinth *		Shared brother's Cub camp visit and demonstrated different layout around central campfire. Helped Josh with chairs. Collected plates and beakers. Suggested testing tents 'to see if they're big enough'.	PSE (DA) 3,5,6,7,8,9 CLL (LCT) 5,6,7,8 CD 3,7,8
Chloe		Selected fabric from box for tents. Helped try to fix it and suggested splitting into groups: 'Let's make two tents and see who can fix it!' Asked for string/scissors and sought help for own idea to tie fabric.	PSE (DA) 3,5,6,7,8,9 PD 3,5 CLL (LCT 5,6,7,8 CD 3,7,8
Observer: Charlotte F.	**Overall summary comments and issues to follow up** The children took charge of their own activity – camping – because greenhouses were beyond their experience and we shall need to attend to this. A lively, imaginative play session where all were involved and delighted in learning! We could set up a real tent outside to build on this and develop MD, KUW		

PHOTOCOPIABLE

Assessing outdoor activities and home- or other play-area sessions

There will be much valuable information to be gathered from observing a range of outdoor and play-area sessions. Outdoor activities are often focused on Physical development, but a great deal of other useful information can also be noted. In many outdoor play situations there will be real opportunities to assess children's responses in Personal, social and emotional development.

Dispositions and attitudes:
➤ an interest in outdoor activities
➤ changing for outdoor activities
➤ involvement in self-initiated activities, choosing apparatus and vehicles
➤ selecting resources independently (small equipment)
➤ trying out and initiating new ideas for games and tasks
➤ perseverance.

Social development:
➤ playing alongside others in games or on the playground area
➤ taking turns for popular or limited vehicles/apparatus
➤ participating in a team or group activity
➤ understanding safety rules and behaving sensibly in outdoor activities.

Emotional development:
➤ separating from adult support and working independently
➤ showing an awareness of own needs and an understanding of how others feel when sharing or waiting for a turn
➤ demonstrating they know the consequences of their own actions.

Useful tip
Use the 'Outdoor-play observation' photocopiable sheet on page 131 as an assessment focus, or to identify areas for provision development.

Useful tip
Use the 'Home role-play observation' photocopiable sheet on page 132. If possible, include a photograph of the child in role – but be careful not to stop the flow of the activity.

There will also be good possibilities for children to further their learning in Communication, language and literacy, as they talk about what they are doing, interact with others and develop their vocabulary in different active situations. In many games activities, skilled practitioners build in an element of Mathematical development, particularly in counting and responding to numbers for moves, or in recognising and making shapes.

For Knowledge and understanding of the world, outdoor activities give excellent opportunities to observe how curious children are about their surroundings, how well they recognise similarities, differences and patterns (such as seasonal change) and how they might use all their senses. Well-planned activities can also provide children with the chance to observe first-hand different colours, textures, shape and form in the natural and made environment and give them experiences which they can later record, supporting aspects of Creative development.

Home-play areas
Most settings will have a special home-play area, if not all the time, then occasionally and fairly regularly. Home-play is universally recognised as an important part of young children's learning, allowing them to role-play different

people and use appropriate vocabulary. It enables them to 'play act' many different situations and work through feelings and ideas arising from their own experience or from other inspirational sources, such as stories and events. The way you provide home-play will depend somewhat on the accommodation your setting enjoys. Some shared premises may result in a more temporary set up where everything has to be packed away at the end of a session, other settings will be able to prepare a more permanent base for home-play. In the most effective settings, the home-play area will be subtly altered from time to time in order to refresh and stimulate children's responses.

In many busy settings, however, practitioners may be too involved to observe home-play activities and staff may be happy to leave children to play on their own. This means that they miss chances both to assess children's progress and to guide their learning. While it would be very difficult to observe every home-play group, staff could realistically plan to observe each child once a half-term in home-play or a similar dedicated role-play task.

Involving children in assessment

An important life skill for everyone is recognising how well they are doing – and to know what steps to take to do even better! When we know clearly our strengths and achievements, even if these are small steps, we can celebrate our successes. The feeling of a good buzz of improvement helps build our self-esteem. This in turn enables us to tackle new, sometimes personally difficult work, learning with increased confidence and the knowledge that we can ultimately succeed.

It is the same with children. Practitioners know that children constantly need reassurance and seek recognition for what they achieve. Young children are usually very eager to demonstrate new skills and demand 'an audience'! All practitioners intuitively know the power of praise in building children's confidence levels and how this encourages them to try out new and challenging experiences. The more a young child can 'bank' successes, the more equipped they will be to learn in the future. This is beautifully exemplified by the child who, when asked by an OFSTED inspector, 'Can you swim?', replied with a beaming smile, 'Yes, but not yet!'

The learning process for children and adults is very much the same. In order to learn new skills we all need to know clearly what we have to do to improve, what any task we are given entails and how to tackle things in manageable steps. Children, therefore, also benefit from knowing what they are learning about, practising or improving, that is, knowing the learning objectives of any activities or tasks that settings offer as part of their programme.

Sharing the learning objectives with children

To involve children in assessment, they need to know first what they are learning! Many very effective settings already have simple systems to involve children in understanding the learning implicit in a range of activities. When the staff plan the coming week's or day's pattern of activities, they discuss the learning objective (what they want the children to know, understand or do) for each task. Staff prepare cards to be displayed by each activity, with the learning objective explained in the children's level of language. For example, a water play activity running for a week with some free-choice and directed groups might have the following cards:

➤ for the youngest children and free-choice activity (where children are encouraged to explore a range of different containers), the card states: 'We are practising pouring and filling and finding out about different things that can hold water.'

➤ For directed group activities for the oldest children, there is more challenge: 'We are finding out which containers hold the most water and putting them in order from most to least'.

Other examples:

➤ For an outdoor activity, children have a group leader with a card on a 'necklace' which states, 'We are looking at, listening for and collecting signs that autumn is here'.

➤ For outdoor play, the practitioner displays a sign by the apparatus, which says, 'We are learning to climb and balance safely.'

➤ For a creative task, 'We are painting our houses' or, 'We are making different coloured patterns'.

➤ For a role-play activity, 'We are cleaning the house' or, 'We are looking after sick animals at the vet's'.

➤ For a mathematical task, 'We are learning to count to six' or, 'We are learning to sort circles and triangles'.

The 'Child's assessment' photocopiable sheet on page 133 has been designed to help you prepare similar cards. The sheet can be cut and used as a paper copy to be placed beside activities, but would be better photocopied onto card and laminated, so that it can be used repeatedly with a dry marker pen. You could easily punch holes in it and attach ribbons. Settings could prepare a bank of these to save time when staff are preparing future work. They can also be sent to parents/carers for home activities.

Organisation

You will need to share the cards with younger children, so that they know what is expected. (Older children should be encouraged to read them for themselves.) This can be done as you explain the range of activities to the children and it will gradually get them used to the system. Also stress that you will ask some of them how well they got on with their learning after they have finished, or when you join their activity.

Realistically, you will not have time for every group to feedback on each activity every session, so it is a good idea to select groups/individuals (on a rolling programme) and let them know that they will report back. You can add a brightly-coloured sticker to learning-objective cards for groups that are going to report back to remind them! Guide the children in their feedback by asking open-ended questions.

Many settings work successfully with a 'Highscope' philosophy, where children 'plan' what they want to do from a range of activities, 'do' their chosen activity and then 'review' what they have done. This system sits well with involving children in assessment, because it encourages independence and responsibility from an early age, reinforcing the learning process very efficiently.

Effective settings share their work with parents/carers and involve children in the process. For example, a nursery school holds regular assembly sessions

Useful tip

Make a note on a large sheet of paper or whiteboard of any ideas or decisions and refer to this the next day to remind the children what was decided.

for specially invited parents/carers. At these events, their children (with staff support) hold up examples of their work in the six Areas of Learning and talk about what they have done, what they have learned and what they want to do next. Where parents/carers have been involved at home, they are encouraged to be part of the presentation too! Photographs are taken of each child and these are added to the child's personal record.

The *Foundation Stage Profile* has a short section which requires discussion with each child. This will be covered in more detail in Chapter 5. Settings that have encouraged children to be involved in their own assessment will find that they are better equipped to share their views with adults. OFSTED inspectors are also charged with asking children about their views, including the youngest ones. Children who are used to working in this way in their everyday work, will be more confident in talking to them!

Sample questions

➤ 'What was your group learning?' (Refer to the card and help them read it.)
➤ 'What did you do?' (Encourage each group member to contribute.)
➤ 'What have you learned/found out?' (Be prepared to give prompts.)
➤ 'What can you do better now?' (Remember to praise their particular successes.)
➤ 'What would you like to do next time?' (Be prepared to offer suggestions and direction.)

The most effective use of staff

To get the maximum benefit, and to use staff skills and expertise to the full, requires careful forward planning. When dealing with assessment issues all staff and helpers can have a real contribution to make. This is because they encounter children at different times and under different circumstances, for example, midday dinner supervisors will work with children in a different environment to their main time in the setting. Often, small children form special relationships with particular staff members, who may not necessarily be their immediate teacher or group leader, and are known very well by them. Children can also present different behaviour or levels of confidence as they react to various adults. In schools, it is likely that children come into contact with a wide range of adults (school secretary, head teacher, caretaker, teachers from other classes, the SENCO and so on) and some of these may have a positive contribution to make to the process. Each setting will need to consider which are the vital personnel that should be included in assessment, or contributing towards it.

Key staff members

In order to manage the assessment process and to keep careful records that are regularly updated, each child should be allocated a key staff member. Ideally, this should be the child's group leader or a member of staff with whom the child has the most contact. In primary schools this is likely to be the teacher (because of their statutory reporting responsibilities), although there should be a strong partnership between the Reception-class teacher and any allocated support staff. A list of key staff and the children they have responsibility for, should be displayed for all staff, visitors and parents/carers.

A key staff member should:

➤ be in charge of maintaining each designated child's records according to the setting's agreed system
➤ check and ensure that allocated children are regularly assessed and their progress tracked in all six Areas of Learning
➤ ensure that observation and assessment of each child is planned into everyday work over time
➤ identify all staff that should positively contribute to the assessment process
➤ ensure all identified staff are clear about their role in the process and know how and when to contribute information
➤ liaise with SENCO to identify children with SEN, supporting Early Years Action and Early Years Action Plus children, being involved in writing and updating Individual Education Plans (IEPs) and in the Annual Review
➤ liaising with other agencies and feeder settings who have assessment data to contribute, also sharing the setting's own assessment information
➤ lead and guide staff discussions on each child's assessment – linked to an agreed rolling programme
➤ meet and discuss children's progress with their parents and carers (possibly in tandem with teachers or those with overall responsibility).

Organisation

This list of tasks will require some time to undertake. Settings need to plan a termly schedule where the different aspects are built into a rolling programme, with some staff meetings earmarked for assessment exchange sessions and collating children's records, so that all staff know when and how they must contribute. It would be useful to have a year planner calendar displayed on the staffroom wall and mark in all the special assessment meetings ahead of time. Add a Post-it Note with details of exactly what is required, which children are in focus and staff roles for each meeting, decided as the year rolls on. Do not conclude a special assessment meeting without completing the detailed Post-it Note for the next important session. Highlight any SEN Reviews and meetings with other agencies and parents in

a distinctive colour, so that staff know that they have to ensure all information is available for these fixed dates. Staff need to put all these dates in their diaries!

Have a central place for records and ensure all staff know how to add any personal observations and assessment information, but stress that key workers need to be aware when items are added. It is useful to have a list clipped to the front cover where staff write the date and content that has been added. For settings where records cannot be left, the key staff member will need to take new information home for collation. It would be useful to have a simple in-tray, into which staff add items at any session, that can be easily transported home. The entire box of records, or selected samples, need only be brought in for the specified assessment meetings.

Special needs support issues

Every setting needs to have a member of staff designated as SENCO, who will take a coordinating role regarding the provision for children with special educational needs and to oversee the implementation of the principles of the *Code of Practice*.

The principles are:

➤ A child with SEN should have their needs met
➤ The SEN of children will normally be met in mainstream schools or settings
➤ The views of the child should be sought and taken into account
➤ Parents/carers have a vital role to play in supporting their child's education
➤ Children with SEN should be offered full access to a broad, balanced and relevant education, including an appropriate curriculum for the Foundation Stage and National Curriculum.

The SENCO should help all staff understand these principles and address them within your setting. They have a leading role, but the SENCO is not expected to take full responsibility for SEN children's education, nor to be their sole teacher. Their role is:

➤ to raise staff awareness of the *Code of Practice* and your setting's responsibilities for Early Years Action (setting-based support) and Early Years Action Plus (the involvement of extra specialist support and local procedures surrounding this)
➤ to help staff use the *Code's* triggers for identifying children with SEN
➤ to offer advice and guidance, and help staff devise interventions that are additional or different from your usual curriculum (such as individual directed work, staff/helper support, additional work with parents, specialist programmes, special resources, adapted equipment) and to formalise these on written IEPs

➤ to ensure that the progress of children with SEN is frequently assessed and recorded and that all staff are aware of the IEP targets and requirements
➤ to coordinate Annual Reviews for children with SEN and liaise with other agencies and pass on assessment information to other providers.

For advice and support on special needs see the series *Special Needs in the Early Years* (Scholastic). Titles include: *Special needs handbook; Speech and language difficulties; Behavioural and emotional difficulties; Learning difficulties; Physical and Coordination difficulties; Medical difficulties; Sensory difficulties* and *Autistic spectrum difficulties.*

Chapter 5 Effective recording

> ➤ **Individual records**
> ➤ **Setting up entry profile records**
> ➤ **Parental involvement**
> ➤ **What to record – gathering information**
> ➤ **Summative recording – Reception classes**
> ➤ **Summative recording – other settings**

Individual records

Every setting will need to set up individual records for each child in its care. The actual form these take is for settings to decide, although it will be important to ensure that certain elements of basic information, however they are designed and arranged, are included. You will need to include:

➤ the child's full name (both legal and known names where these differ. With so many variations in family structures, it will be important to have accurate information and to know the correct titles for parents and carers as well as for the child)
➤ date of birth (primary schools will also generally require to see children's birth certificates)
➤ address and telephone (and with whom the child normally resides)
➤ any access arrangements (it is important to establish this in split families and to know if this is a legal or an informal arrangement)
➤ who will normally deliver and collect the child
➤ emergency contact address and telephone (and relationship of contact to child, for example, father, aunt, neighbour)
➤ the child's mother tongue (if applicable) and parents'/carers' preferred language for communications (if this can be arranged)
➤ any special medical issues (asthma, eczema, allergies, other conditions requiring medication or attention)
➤ any physical conditions (glasses, hearing, disabilities, mobility or other issues)
➤ any previously identified SEN and agencies that may be involved in support
➤ the date of entry to your setting
➤ previous settings attended (with dates if possible).

Other useful information, which is best gleaned from personal and private discussions with parents/carers includes:

➤ the child's position in the family (youngest, oldest, and so on)
➤ names of any brothers and sisters, particularly those attending your setting
➤ the child's special interests, likes and skills (for example: uses a computer at home, loves animals)
➤ the child's dislikes (for example: foods and drinks they have an aversion to, whether they are fearful of dogs or rough play)

➤   names of the child's special friends
➤   the child's favourite toys and games
➤   any family pets and their names
➤   any special family information and interests (for example: grandparents in India, mum is a skilled artist, dad is a fire-fighter – information to help you make the child feel special and which may be helpful to you for involving the family in your setting!)
➤   other specific issues raised by parents or carers.

You will also then need to include space for ongoing assessments of progress, which directly refer to the six Areas of Learning. You should find many of the photocopiable sheets in this book useful to help you complete thorough records. In particular, refer to the 'Individual record title page' photocopiable sheet on page 134.

Security matters

Parents and carers are understandably often concerned about the security of their child's records and who will have access to them. Your setting needs to have a clear policy on this issue and you should assure parents/carers that all records will be kept securely, with access only by practitioners. If you have many voluntary helpers and parents/carers in your setting, you need to consider how any contributions they make towards assessment and children's record-keeping will be dealt with. One way that they can continue to make a valuable contribution with their own observations and comments is simply to ensure that they complete all observation forms, Post-it Notes and so on (as per your arrangements), but that each child's key staff member is responsible for collating and maintaining the actual records.

Case history

In one successful nursery, the agreed policy is for all records to be the personal property of the parents and the child. Each child has a record book, with their name and a large photograph on the cover (taken by staff). These are kept securely on racks in the setting and the parents and children can have easy access to them. Children and practitioners refer to them together in the normal course of their work and any child can ask for a specific piece of work they are proud of, or a photograph, to be added to it. Other agencies, including OFSTED inspectors, have to ask the parents' and children's permission to look at them. In practice this works very well. Parents and children greatly value the records, are proud of the content and trust the practitioners, so refusal to share information is rare! When the child moves on, a summary record is passed to the Reception-class teachers and the parents and children are presented with their original record book to take home.

You should ensure parents/carers know that it is good early years practice to take photographs of children as part of your setting's normal work, for record-keeping purposes and to share with OFSTED inspectors to show the full range of your provision. Reassure them that the photographs stay in the setting and are not available to the public.

Useful tip
Although most parents will be happy to give you information about their child, remember that some of it could be sensitive.
➤   Always try to meet the parents personally and establish a warm professional climate in which to discuss the questions together.
➤   Avoid sending out forms 'cold' because this gives the wrong message.

Personalising your records

All settings are unique and it is appropriate to make your individual records as personal to your setting as possible. Add your own logos and specific designs to any forms. This makes them less daunting for parents/carers and children and generally more attractive to use. Reception classes can also personalise their record systems, so long as information can be ultimately transferred to the *Foundation Stage Profile* scales by the end of the year, and that this form of information is shared with parents/carers.

Setting up entry profile records

The previous section offered you guidance about the elements that need to be present in each child's record, beginning with the information that needs to be gathered in order to start the process. The 'Individual record title page' photocopiable sheet on page 134 is a useful model for the cover page for each child's record, and can be adapted and decorated to personalise it for each child and for your setting.

Useful tip

Let parents have photographs of their children that are no longer required – they can make very welcome calendars and Christmas gifts – or charge a small fee to cover costs and swell funds!

Getting ready – a checklist

➤ Decide what format your records will take (files, ring-binders, home-made booklets or loose sheets in a plastic wallet) and how these will be stored securely and confidentially.

➤ Discuss with staff and agree the style of forms and inclusions for the profile. (This book offers many time-saving photocopiable sheets, or you can adapt these ideas for your own use.)

➤ Agree the timetable for first observations – although settings will naturally be anxious to give new children attention to help them settle in, it is advisable to allow at least two weeks before making the first formalised observations to judge entry attainment.

➤ Determine which staff members will observe which children and how long observation periods will be (ideally fairly short initially).

➤ Set up the date for a feedback meeting for staff to report on all observations they have undertaken and to seek the views of other staff.

➤ Schedule dates for staff to meet with parents to share the information on how their children have settled and how they have presented in all of the six Areas of Learning.

➤ Before a child joins your setting, arrange how you will obtain basic information from the child's parents or carers. Undertake these discussions and record the relevant information. You may find the 'Parent's entry contribution' photocopiable sheet on page 135 and the following section entitled 'Parental involvement' helpful.

➤ Where a child has attended a previous setting, you should try to obtain any available assessment information and add this to the child's record.

➤ Similarly, where a child has been involved with other agencies (for example, health services) or has been identified as having SEN, obtain all necessary information from the relevant sources.

It will also be beneficial for you to read 'Entry assessment' in Chapter 3, before embarking on this section. Much of the advice in that earlier passage is concerned with the management issues of obtaining preliminary information. It is designed to complement this section, which is concerned with making initial judgements about each child's attainment on entry and contains a practical suggestion checklist for implementation. The 'Early days assessment' photocopiable sheet on page 114 offers a compact format which your staff may find helpful to use for observations of children in the first few weeks of their entry to your setting.

After initial observations

➤ After staff discussions, finalise views on each new child's entry attainment in the six Areas of Learning and note this in their personal entry profile.
➤ Consider how your setting will meet the learning needs identified by any observations made.
➤ Hold meetings for parents and primary carers and sensitively discuss how their child is settling in. Introduce the child's record, discuss the things they are doing, how your setting will help them make progress and ways in which parents/carers can use home links to support the child's learning.

Parental involvement

Effective early years settings have always recognised the importance of parents and carers as partners in children's learning. When parents/carers and practitioners work together positively in early years settings, the results have a significant impact on children's overall development and their capacity to learn successfully.

Developing the parental relationship

School settings are required to develop a dialogue with parents and carers early in the Reception year, when the practitioner with responsibility for completing the *Foundation Stage Profile* should seek parents/carers' views on any relevant aspects of their child's development observed outside the setting.

However, this is good practice for all settings and is the first step in involving parents/carers in the assessment process. As such, it must be handled with warmth and sensitivity. Parents/carers need to feel at ease, have confidence in your setting and feel valued as important partners in their child's learning. Get this stage wrong and you will have to work very hard to regain parental trust! It is worth investing staff-training time to clarify the process and share best practice before you begin to establish these relationships with parents/carers.

Two photocopiable sheets have been designed to help staff gather and share information. The 'Parents' entry contribution' photocopiable sheet on page 135 is a model for initial discussions with new parents/carers. The 'Parents' ongoing contribution' photocopiable sheet on page 136 is designed as an agenda for parental discussions and for reporting a summary of their child's progress. It also contains a section for you to add agreed new targets for learning, which can be either setting or home-support targets.

Streamlining your parental relationship for assessment

Consider the following steps to a productive partnership:

Initial meetings
➤ Hold discussions with all staff to stress the importance of initial contacts and share ways to make parents feel at ease with the process.
➤ Set up your parental discussion schedule.
➤ Earmark a private place for discussions and have toys and games to occupy children while you talk.
➤ Ensure that any forms you complete are attractively presented and non-threatening to parents/carers. Explain that the completion of these is to help your setting get to know the child better and to help the child get the most out of the time at your setting.

➤ Show the child's record book (or similar) to parents/carers, explaining that this will be frequently discussed with them and their contributions will form an important part.
➤ Reception classes should briefly introduce parents/carers to the *Foundation Stage Profile* and explain how and when this will be used.
➤ Try to complete forms in a relaxed manner. Do not bombard parents/carers with the questions, but introduce them in a conversational way. You could then read out anything you have written for confirmation.
➤ If parents/carers raise queries or concerns that you cannot deal with immediately, agree to get back to them and follow these up as soon as possible.
➤ Look at back-up systems for parents/carers who are unavailable. Try to arrange alternative dates and times. For example, one good setting plans an evening session every term (after a staff takeaway supper) to meet the few parents/carers who cannot come at other times!
➤ Consider telephone discussions for parents/carers you cannot see in person (but rehearse what you are going to say beforehand so that you are not diverted). Sending out forms 'cold' is not recommended but, if this is unavoidable, be sure that your covering letter is warm in tone and gives telephone contacts in case parents/carers have queries.
➤ Share the pattern for all subsequent parental discussions, explaining how you will discuss their children's progress together. Ensure that parents/carers realise this is additional to the informal contact between staff parents/carers which takes place on a daily basis.

Follow-up meetings
➤ At subsequent discussions, prepare information about attendance, health and behaviour as well as the child's significant successes in all six Areas of Learning.
➤ Pencil in the 'next steps' (or most appropriate new targets for learning)

in specific aspects of the six Areas of Learning, including ways in which the parents/carers can support this at home. When these are agreed, complete them in a bright-coloured pen, so they stand out for early discussion at the next parents' meeting.

➤ Encourage parents/carers to contribute their own views, if necessary prompting them with questions such as, 'What does he talk about at home?' or, 'What does she like best at our setting?'

➤ Have the previous record of your meeting handy and report on any progress in the listed learning targets. Be swift to congratulate parents/carers on their home link support and the difference it makes to children's learning. If it was not

Checklist for your record-keeping system

➤ Is it personalised and user-friendly?

➤ Does it give a clear picture of each child's progress from their entry to the setting until the current time?

➤ Will it help new staff get to know the child better? How?

➤ Will it help staff in their planning for individual children? How could it be used for this purpose?

➤ Will it especially show the effects of the support given to children with SEN, be helpful for the SENCO checking progress, and be valuable for drawing up IEPs and for Annual Reviews?

➤ Will it be useful for any other agencies involved with the child? Will it show whether there is progress in English as an additional language?

➤ Is it firmly based on different layers of information, which can easily be added to and extended?

➤ Does it include:
  • basic entry information, discussed and agreed with parents?
  • an early assessment of the child in the setting (based on staff assessments), so that attainment on entry to the setting can be seen?
  • scheduled and regular observations recorded by staff to an agreed format, which are added as the child moves through the setting?
  • records of ongoing discussions with the parents and their views?
  • any targets for learning and home-link support?
  • records of discussions with the children and their views?
  • photographs of the child engaged in activities and/or their work?
  • examples of work, including those selected by the child?
  • Post-its, notes, tapes and other useful information?
  • evidence of progress clearly indicated in all six Areas of Learning?

➤ If completing a *Foundation Stage Profile* for each child, does the system give enough evidence to do this?

➤ Are records shared with parents and children as the children progress through the setting?

➤ Is it manageable, with programmed times for adding information? Is there a rolling programme or set dates for specific sections to be completed?

➤ Is it becoming too bulky? Is it possible to check that any retained evidence is still essential? If too much has been collected, could important points be summarised and the files thinned out?

successful, do not be critical, but be sure to suggest some new ideas for them to
follow up next time!
➤ Reception classes will need to report on the *Foundation Stage Profile* at the
end of the summer term.

What to record – gathering information

Every setting needs to develop an effective record-keeping system that is
designed to give a clear picture of each child's progress and development over
time. Whilst there is no prescribed format for how this should look, your system
should contain enough information to be useful to practitioners and to support
children's further learning. You will need to decide the style of record-keeping
that will be the most manageable and useful for your setting. The detailed
advice in Chapter 3 should be a helpful guide.

When deciding or reviewing your system, work through the following list of
questions. If you can give positive answers to these, your system is likely to be
effective. If there are any negative responses, consider what action you need
to take, over time, to include any missing areas. Plan to review your system
every year or so to ensure that it still meets your needs, matches any new
requirements and that you incorporate any good ideas from staff to make it
work better for you!

Recording information in the six Areas of Learning

It will be important for all settings to record what
children have learned within all six Areas of Learning in
order to give a rounded picture of overall attainment. It
is quite possible for a child to do better in some areas
than others, or to have a particular facility for an Area of
Learning because of previous experiences.

The 'Six Areas of Learning – assessment focus
sheet' photocopiable sheets on pages 115–127, which
accompany the guidance in Chapter 3, have been
designed for use both in making observations of
children at work and also for recording their attainment.
Practitioners should find that this dual design makes
the process of assessment and record-keeping more
manageable and requires less paperwork! If a full set of
these sheets is added to each child's record, staff can
record their judgements over time.

Recording judgements

Most experienced staff will be able to recall from their own knowledge of
each child many elements of attainment, particularly for the earlier levels.
For instance, when considering children's attainment in Personal, social and
emotional development – Social development, most practitioners will know
from their day-to-day interaction with individual children whether they, 'Play
alongside others', Build relationships through gesture and talk' and, 'Take turns
and share with adult support' (the first three elements on the *Profile* scale).

Staff will probably find the same is true for many other examples of the first
three elements within other Areas of Learning. Consequently, it should be
relatively easy to rapidly confirm whether each child demonstrates these skills

and for this to be recorded at a staff meeting. A key member of staff could simply ask staff their views, confirm the judgement and date the record.

Some of the more advanced elements in the six Areas of Learning may be easily tackled in the same way, but there will be a definite need for proper observations to decide on a child's attainment in many of them. Attainment for the majority of the five next stages (deemed to be around the average child's attainment by the end of the Foundation Stage) should be measured by more than one observation to ensure that judgements are really secure. For example, to continue focusing on PSED – Social development, practitioners would want to have more than one example of a child respecting people's views, cultures and beliefs to record that this was securely attained. Where several staff can cite good examples over a period of time, the key staff member may feel confident to record a positive judgement. Where evidence is thin, perhaps because staff have not had opportunities to observe this in a child's activities, a special focus needs to be set up so that a future decision can be made.

It should also be remembered that the different elements are not always hierarchical. Staff can agree and record attainment in less, or more, advanced elements, as each child presents. However, remember that the final, ninth element on the scale is to record where a child consistently operates at this higher level. For judgements to be really secure here, staff should have significant evidence from several different sources (and preferably more than one practitioner). In the same PSED – Social development example, a child who, 'Takes into account the ideas of others' (element 9) would do so consistently, as his or her normal response to others; occasional or intermittent examples would not confirm this level of attainment.

Exceptional children – 'gifted and talented'

For rare cases where your setting has exceptional children, further assessments may also apply. For example in PSED, this might apply to children who are demonstrating amazing maturity and levels of leadership, with an exceedingly high degree of confidence and personal responsibility that they are almost autonomous learners. In this case, your setting would need to record evidence of this, through observations and staff comments.

The photocopiable sheets throughout this book could still be used effectively, so long as practitioners write clearly (preferably using a brightly-coloured pen) that, 'This child is operating at an exceptional level, far beyond that generally expected for his/her age'. In some Areas of Learning, such as mathematics, settings that are familiar with National Curriculum standards, may be able to offer specific evidence of the 'best match' level of attainment. In these cases, it would be wise to confer with a Key Stage 1 colleague or teacher mentor to moderate your judgements.

If your setting is using the *Foundation Stage Profile* for recording purposes, you will need to place a tick in the appropriate circle – the one marked 'Further assessment applies'.

Children with identified special educational needs

For those children who join your setting with known special educational needs, you should have some early assessment evidence from other agencies and sources to include with your records. Some children may already have an outline IEP, which your setting needs to take account of in planning the child's support programme. This needs to be included but, more importantly, discussed with all staff who will engage with the child, so that everyone is clear on the major focus of support and can reinforce any learning targets that have been set. You can still use the photocopiable sheets throughout this book to record staff observations and progress checks, but you will need to supplement these with any other SEN records that may be required by your local education authority and also a good sample of each child's work.

Where children are causing you some concern and it is your setting that has identified possible SEN, you can use the photocopiable sheets in this book as the basis of your record-keeping. However, as you will often need to share evidence with other agencies before decisions on extra support or special provision can be made, it is advisable to retain a greater selection of these children's work to show other professionals.

If your setting is using the *Foundation Stage Profile* for recording children's attainment and it is not possible to record positive assessments for any elements of the scales, you will need to place a tick in the 'Alternative assessment applies' circle.

Retaining samples of children's work

In addition to the records that you can build up using the photocopiable models throughout this book, it will be useful to collect samples of characteristic work that give a 'feel' for the attainment and progress each child is making over time. For example, early mark-making or 'writing' from a doctor's surgery role-play activity could be added to 'Communication, language and literacy – Writing'. At a later date a further sample of emergent writing, perhaps children writing their own names or a greetings card, could be added. Where settings send most work home, photocopies could be made, or children asked to show parents/carers their work with you present and then pass it on for inclusion in their record file. If the sample is very large, or a bulky or delicate piece of artwork or a model, photographs can be used very effectively.

Many settings successfully involve children in the selecting of samples as part of their normal assessment processes. In one setting, children have individual discussions with their key staff member about once each half-term. During this time they look together at the work samples in the record book and talk about how well the child is doing and what they are going to work at next. The child can also help select other examples of work to go into the record. Where work is chosen in this way, staff write on it, 'Selected by_____ because_____' and so make the task part of a learning activity. The record files and work samples are shared with parents/carers at parental meetings and staff find this a very good focus for discussions about children's progress. Parents/carers also enjoy seeing their children's work and can clearly see progress (or, occasionally, concerns) for themselves.

In another setting, children know that they can ask staff at any time to put a piece of work they are proud of in their file, or take a photograph of it for later inclusion. As with the previous example, the children have to dictate a comment to staff to say why they are especially pleased with this work, but also what they had learned by doing it!

In one Reception-class setting children can request the use of the school's digital camera and are taught to take their own photographs for later inclusion in their records. When the photographs are printed, the teacher plans activities for the children to write their own annotations, answering the questions on a prompt card:

I am_____
I have chosen this for my file because I'm proud of the way I_____
To do even better, next time I shall_____

Samples chosen by staff can be added to a child's file, but these should be very carefully annotated and dated so as to give the context and help staff gauge progress when reviewing different samples obtained over time.
The annotations should make clear:

➤ the nature of the task
➤ whether it was a group or individual activity
➤ whether the child was supported or unaided
➤ any strengths (what the child could do)
➤ particular difficulties (what the child could not do)
➤ any quotes/comments from the child
➤ any quotes/comments from support staff.

Obtaining children's views

There are many ways that children should be involved in the assessment process. 'Involving the children in assessment' in Chapter 4 gives guidance on how children can be involved in assessing their day-to-day learning. This section is concerned with how children can be involved in staged discussions about their learning and in sharing and recording their views.

The importance of involving children fully in the assessment process is to help them develop their ability to express preferences and make choices, begin to understand that their personal views are respected and help them develop as independent learners.

Even young children can be beneficially involved in talking to trusted staff about their likes and dislikes. As a beginning to the process a practitioner can engage a child in conversation. By gently prompting children to talk about things they feel confident in (favourite toys, their pets, things they do at home), the practitioner can succeed in getting them to relax and respond. Sometimes children need time to consider their answers, and skilled staff will wait patiently, with encouraging and attentive body language, until the child is ready to speak.

Prompting children's responses

For very young children, using a puppet or special toy can be a helpful focus. One playgroup setting has introduced an appealing rag doll called Shy Sarah. Staff explain that Shy Sarah is feeling a bit nervous about being at the setting and they ask the children to whisper their answers to the questions 'to make Sarah feel happier' – and the children respond enthusiastically!

Another nursery setting has a huge fluffy kitten that is only used when children's discussions are held. Each child is given the toy to stroke and enjoy during the discussions, so that the occasion is seen to be very special. The other children also know that this is a sign not to interrupt. The setting also uses the

Examples of involving children to help develop self-reflection skills include:

➤ staff asking children at the end of an activity whether they enjoyed it and which parts they liked the most
➤ staff helping children to identify why they enjoyed or did not enjoy an event
➤ children responding with 'thumbs-up' or 'thumbs-down' signs after an activity or task
➤ children holding up 'smiley' or 'unsmiley' faces (on cards or as lolly-stick puppets) at the end of an activity
➤ each child having a laminated card, divided into boxes. The child draws a picture in each box of the activity they chose (or was directed towards) to plan what they will do. After the activity they draw a 'smiley face' for a successful session or an 'unsmiley face' for one they did not feel went well
➤ Reception-class children having traffic-light cards (one green, one amber/orange, one red). At the end of each task they are asked to choose a card to hold up:
Green = I enjoyed it and learned what I should have done/could do
Amber/orange = I enjoyed it and I am beginning to learn, but need more practice
Red = This did not go so well. I need more help.

Useful tip
Self-reflection activities help to create a secure and comfortable atmosphere. It is a small step then to setting up productive one-to-one discussions.

kitten on recording sheets to reinforce the connection. The children quickly see this as a normal activity and are confident and relaxed. Some even tell staff that they are 'saving things up to tell Kitty'!

In one busy Reception-class setting, the teacher has made a large wooden 'lollipop tree' sign on a stand. On this is printed '_____'s special time'. The teacher adds a child's name (on a card) and takes the child to a quiet corner for short discussions, and the other children know not to disturb them.

Recording children's own views and assessments

There are many ways in which children can be involved in their own assessments on a day-to-day basis, which help build their confidence and make it easier for them to discuss their own views. Settings which introduce ways for children to reflect on what they are doing, what they are learning and to express personal likes and dislikes in a socially acceptable manner, help children become familiar with this process.

To be most useful, an initial discussion with children should be planned to take place after a few weeks of their joining your setting. Ideally the discussions should be led by the member of staff who has most contact with the child. The 'Child's record sheet – early days' photocopiable sheet on page 137 has been designed to help staff undertake this activity. The sheet can be filled in alongside the child, but if this is likely to inhibit their responses, use the headings as an agenda and complete the form at a later time. Some settings may like the children to colour in the illustrations and smiley faces, so that the children have some form of ownership. You can also ask the child to draw their responses in the boxes and then act as scribe to describe their pictures. The sheet can be referred to at the next one-to-one discussion and gives a good focus for practitioners to talk about how children have settled in well and made progress.

It is also a useful framework to share with parents/carers who want to know how well their child has settled.

The 'Child's record sheet – ongoing' photocopiable sheet on page 138 is designed to be used when the child is well-settled and thoroughly familiar with your setting. This should be discussed and completed alongside the child, who can respond as before with drawings, dictating to staff, or attempting to write in their own way with appropriate levels of support. Again, the form can be coloured in if desired. This second form can be used several times to update children's views, and previous sheets can be compared to illustrate and discuss changes and progress.

Reception-class settings can use the sheet as a basis for collecting the information from discussions with children, which can then be summarised and transferred to the *Foundation Stage Profile* in due course.

Summative recording – Reception classes

The Foundation Stage is recognised as a statutory stage of the National Curriculum for England, alongside Key Stages 1–4, although interestingly, the statutory age for compulsory attendance at school remains at the term after children reach their fifth birthday! Recent and welcome expansions of early years funded provision for three- and four-year-old children has resulted in most children entering school with time spent in other foundation settings. This means that Reception classes may have intakes that have had many different forms of earlier provision and could include children whose parents or primary carers have opted for no previous formal provision.

The *Foundation Stage Profile* replaces the former statutory Baseline Assessment that was made on entry to the primary school. Its function is to be a summary record of each child's attainment by the end of the Foundation Stage, assessed against a national benchmark of scales within each of the six Areas of Learning.

Schools are free to continue to use their own internal assessment systems, or devise new ones to complement the final use of the *Foundation Stage Profile*. Practitioners will certainly need to carry out accurate observations and make carefully considered judgements, gathering secure evidence over time, on individual children's levels of attainment. Such information will be essential for staff to cover the different elements of the *Foundation Stage Profile* booklet. Whatever system is used, the completion of the *Foundation Stage Profile* for each child by the end of the summer term in the Reception class is now a requirement.

School responsibilities

The head teacher and governors are charged with responsibility for:

➤ ensuring that the *Foundation Stage Profile* is duly completed for each child according to national requirements
➤ arranging for practitioners with responsibility for completion of the

Foundation Stage Profile to take part in local authority moderation activities at least once every year.

➤ permitting local authority moderators to visit the setting to carry out moderation activities

➤ meeting reasonable requests from the moderator to adjust any assessments where this is deemed necessary

➤ facilitating practitioners to take part in further training or moderation activities where this will help their professional development.

All the photocopiable sheets in this book have been designed to help practitioners gather information on children's attainment. They can form the core of an assessment system for a Reception class, because they are tightly linked to the various requirements of the *Foundation Stage Profile*. In particular, the 'Six Areas of Learning – assessment focus sheet' photocopiable sheets on pages 115–127 have been drawn up to cover the sub-divisions in PSED, CLL and Mathematical development. These should provide a useful framework for busy practitioners and ensure that they can amass information, in a measured way over time, which will help with the completion of the summary *Foundation Stage Profile* six Areas of Learning sections adequately.

Bite-sized chunks...

The old adage, 'It's best to eat an elephant in bite-sized chunks' is so true in tackling the *Foundation Stage Profile*! It is sensible for practitioners to collect valuable evidence and significant samples of children's work and retain these, but it is not essential to collect vast quantities. Remember that the *Foundation Stage Profile* is a summary of your considered judgements.

Complete the section 'Information about the child from previous settings' as soon as you have this – ask your head teacher to chase up any missing elements. Fill in 'Discussion with parents (1)' at the first half-term. Then, at the end of each term, meet with the other Reception-class practitioners and consider all the gathered evidence together. If you are a lone Reception teacher ask your early years coordinator to work with you, or consider linking with another lone Reception-class colleague in your area. You could ask your teacher mentor or moderator to arrange links. Consider the examples and evidence to date and complete the *Foundation Stage Profile* scales for the current term wherever you can, making notes and comments in the specified sections as appropriate. Add your comments under 'Discussion with parents (2)' and final summer-term child discussions after these have taken place (see the 'Parents' entry contribution' photocopiable sheet on page 135 and 'Parents' ongoing contribution' photocopiable sheet on page 136 for useful starting-points).

You can then choose the most suitable action for your setting's circumstances.

These might be:

➤ to retain the samples of work as they are in each child's record, for distribution at the end of the year

➤ to clip reviewed evidence together and store it elsewhere, but retain it to pass on to parents/carers, colleagues and other agencies at the end of the year

➤ to retain the samples of work for moderation purposes and to share with visiting moderators

➤ to keep only the most vital evidence and send other examples home to the parents/carers after each termly collation.

English as an additional language

Many children in settings come from homes where English is not the first language. Some children can be fluent in more than one language, but not yet in English! The *Foundation Stage Profile* contains an important section for noting children's attainment in English as an additional language. If children's early language development is in a language other than English, it is vital that you find out as much as possible about this. Language development in English and the home language complement and support each other.

You should record the following:

➤ which language(s) a child understands and/or speaks

➤ whether the child uses different languages with different people

➤ what language experience a child has in the home language (rhymes, songs, stories and so on)

➤ whether the child is learning to read and write in their home language, and if so, how

➤ what, if any, additional specialist support the child receives

➤ the general progress noted in English acquisition.

If bilingual support is available, you can complete all other sections of the *Profile* in the normal way, except CLL scales 4–9 which must be assessed in English.

Summative recording – other settings

Although only Reception classes are currently charged with the responsibility for completing the *Foundation Stage Profile* as each child reaches the end of their Reception year, all settings will need to have their own assessment and record-keeping systems. All settings need to pass on a summary of children's attainment and previous experience to the next providers. The *Foundation Stage Profile* includes a special section – the very first in the document – entitled 'Information about the child from previous settings'. Reception staff will need to complete this to give a brief outline of each child's background context to previous learning. They will need your information in order to do it effectively.

Identifying the next providers

It will be useful for you to compile a contact list of schools or other providers that your children move on to. You can ask parents/carers to say where their children will go next and school addresses can be found in the telephone directory for your area. For other settings, you may need to consult your local education authority Early Years' Partnership manager, your teacher mentor, or the library. If possible, make contact with the settings the majority of your children go on to and try to find a named contact.

You can be pro-active and send invitations to other providers to visit your setting and meet your staff informally – tea and cakes usually help generate a relaxed atmosphere! Remember that brief lunchtime meetings and after normal school hours will be easier for Reception- and nursery-class teachers to manage and this may also be true for other providers.

If meetings are not possible, send out a letter to identified providers (or a blanket letter to all possible providers) giving brief information about your setting. Let them know:

➤   your setting's full title, nature, address and the name of the manager or contact member of staff
➤   the times and sessions you meet
➤   the provision you offer and the range of ages and numbers of children
➤   that you believe that several, or many of your children will transfer to their setting at a later stage
➤   that you will want to send summary information to them of transferring children to help them get to know their new children and to know what previous learning and experiences they have had
➤   that you can also enclose a copy of the summary assessment sheet in due course (see further guidance below).

Organising your assessment information for other providers

Your setting will have gathered a great deal of information about each child over time. The range of photocopiable sheets in this book can help you build up a core framework for assessment. The 'Six Areas of Learning – assessment focus sheet' photocopiable sheets on pages 115–127, linked as they are to the Stepping Stones and Early Learning Goals for the Foundation Stage, should be particularly helpful. The sheets have been designed to match the full Areas of Learning, with the additional sub-divisions for Personal, social and emotional development, Communication, language and literacy, and Mathematical development, as per the *Foundation Stage Profile*, which must be completed by the end of the Reception year.

Using these as a basis for assessment in your setting will help you gather and pass on information that will be directly beneficial to the children, by helping your school-based colleagues plan appropriately matched work for them. Your information will also help teachers begin the *Foundation Stage Profile* accurately. The first three elements of each of these photocopiable sheets relate mainly to the Stepping Stones in the *Curriculum Guidance for the Foundation Stage*. They describe a child who is still progressing towards the Early Learning Goals. It is likely, therefore, that settings catering for the youngest children will be recording attainment for the majority of their children in these elements, although some children may attain some higher elements because of general ability or previous learning experiences.

Settings catering for older children are likely to observe attainment over a greater range.

You will probably have collected a good selection of other information, including direct observations, parent and child discussion notes, photographs of activities and samples of children's work. Some settings will present each child's record file, with the photographs and work sample, as a leaving gift. Some settings ask parents/carers to take these on to the new setting to pass to receiving staff. Other settings retain their records in case of any further enquiries. Passing on the entire record on its own, although often delightful, is not always helpful to busy practitioners who need to assimilate information swiftly and plan new learning programmes. Ideally, send the records with any samples you feel appropriate, but include a summary sheet, which highlights the most significant points you want new staff to know about. This should guarantee the most important aspects are read first!

Preparing a summary sheet

The 'Passing on information' photocopiable sheet on page 139 has been designed as a model to help you encapsulate the key information points in a manageable manner. There are three distinct sections. The top section gives the child's basic details, plus your setting's contact. It also lets you share information on general attendance and health issues, which a new setting would need to know. Importantly, it has space for you to inform them of a child's preferred activities and also names any special friends. Knowing this will help practitioners talk to the child in informed way and tailor some initial activities or groupings to help with settling in.

The second section has boxes for all six Areas of Learning. These should be completed with the most significant attainments or concerns for each Area of Learning. If you are including more detailed records, this can be mentioned in the appropriate box or on the relevant line underneath. The final section gives space for other important comments such as special educational needs issues or other issues which may affect the child.

Receiving staff at the new setting would be happy with such an accessible summary and would know how to look into other attached records or follow up any queries directly with you. Having a standard system such as this also means that new settings are familiar with your record keeping system.

Chapter 6 Involving others

> ➤ **Who should be involved in assessment?**
> ➤ **Observation techniques**
> ➤ **Involving staff fully**
> ➤ **Involving helpers effectively**
> ➤ **Making the most of parents'/carers' involvement**
> ➤ **Working positively with other agencies**

Who should be involved in assessment?

Children will have a wide variety of early years learning experience. Some will have enjoyed extensive time in one or more different settings, such as playgroups and nursery settings, whereas others may have spent most of their time at home, or with child minders and family carers. However children have been cared for, and wherever they have been involved in learning, they will have been observed – even if only informally – by different adults. As children mature, these adults will have noticed their general growth, their emerging personalities and their developing abilities to do an increasing number of things. They will also have noticed the things that the children continue to find difficult or where help is needed. Adults with close regular contact with children may have also noticed any physical difficulties, such as vision or hearing concerns, and alerted parents/carers or sought specialist attention.

Grandparents often give their own children guidance based on their own child-rearing experience. However, current family and work-mobility patterns often mean that young parents do not have the same access to their extended families as was once the case. Young parents are not always sure what to expect as their children mature, particularly with a first child. The range of health professionals and adults organising toddler groups, playgroups and nursery settings may be the ones they turn to for advice, because they recognise that these adults have a wider experience of young children throughout their growth and development.

The *Foundation Stage Profile handbook* (QCA) is very clear that many different adults have a role to play in providing valuable assessment information. It states: 'As judgements are based on observational evidence from a wide range of learning and teaching contexts, it is expected that all those adults who interact with the child in the setting will contribute to the process and that account will be taken, both of assessments made during the first year of the Foundation Stage, and of information provided by parents/carers.'

This has particular importance for schools, which do not have nursery provision and where children are admitted directly to Reception classes. In these cases children are joining their setting halfway through the Foundation Stage. It will be crucial for these schools to endeavour to gain as much information as possible from other settings that their new intake has attended, as well as liaising very closely with parents/carers who can provide significant information. All schools are required to complete the formal *Foundation Stage Profile* by the end of the Reception class and to share this information with parents/carers. There are also important sections that must be completed, covering information about the child from previous settings and discussions with parents or carers.

Clearly there are many sources of valuable information which need tapping into, but with careful management. Realistically it will be impossible, and totally unwieldy, to seek out and involve all the adults that have been concerned in a child's early learning experiences. However, there are some key sources, which should be explored. These include gaining information from:

➤ parents and carers
➤ the previous setting (or settings, if the child has attended more than one concurrently, for example, one in the mornings and another in the afternoons)
➤ other agencies, such as health or social services.

Information from parents and carers

Parents and carers have a vital and unique knowledge of aspects of their children's early development, which is central to the assessment process. They can also tell you where other important information can be gathered. They can supply the contact information for any settings their child has attended previously, and any health or other agencies that may have been involved, which you will need to follow up. However, you should be very sensitive about seeking this information and reassure parents/carers that it is only to help you support their child better, that all records are secure and that staff treat such matters professionally and confidentially. You should ask parents/carers to share any individual record books or children's work that other settings have given them. Some settings pass these to parents and encourage them to take them to their new setting.

Try to build a warm and productive relationship with parents/carers from the start. Remember the initial contact is crucial to the success of the partnership. Stress that you value parents'/carers' contributions and that there will be many regular opportunities to work together and discuss their children's progress in your setting. You will find 'Making the most of parents'/carers' involvement' later in this chapter gives more detailed guidance.

Information from previous settings

Parents/carers should give you the names and addresses of previous settings for you to follow up. Personal contact with providers is generally the most beneficial way to gain professional trust and obtain the most useful entry information. Settings will usually have their own internal records and may be happy to give these to you. However, they may be grateful for some guidance about the type of information you need. The 'Passing on information' photocopiable sheet on page 139 might be a helpful form to pass on for colleague practitioners to use.

Information from other agencies

Again, this can be a sensitive area and you will need parents/carers to give you the information. This is best approached through relaxed discussions about the child's general health and any special medical or physical issues that your setting needs to support. You should be professionally reassuring about security, stressing that any information is to help your setting meet their child's needs and that you want to work in partnership with parents, carers and all involved services. You should not independently contact other agencies to enquire whether a child is 'on the books' – you need parents'/carers' agreement or you can respond to direct contacts from the agencies concerned. If you have concerns once the child is attending your setting, you need to discuss this firstly with the parents/carers, obtain agreement and support the parents/carers as you follow it up. Parents/carers can be very anxious, sometimes in denial, and your support and open-partnership role may be crucial in allaying their fears, and ultimately helping their child make progress.

Observation techniques

Observation is at the very heart of accurate assessment. Most practitioners absorb information from their general interactions with children every day, and are aware of children's varied responses and developmental stages. If they are asked to recall how a particular child reacts during activities they have led, staff can usually have a picture in their mind of the child's contribution. However, most practitioners are also extremely busy people and it can be difficult to guarantee them observing children intently as they engage in many different activities. It is so easy to be sidetracked in a hectic environment!

It is sometimes difficult to ensure that staff have opportunities to carry out observations of the full spectrum of children's activities and this is especially true in settings where there is limited extra help available, for example, in Reception classes where extra support may not be full-time. In these cases, it will be vital to plan observations of different groups or individuals over a suitable length of time and also ensure that any available support staff have a clear idea of how they can contribute to the process.

Often busy staff are locked into working so intensely on activities with groups or individuals they find it almost impossible to observe free-play or role-play, which they tend to leave because they are so involved elsewhere. This means that they miss very telling examples of how young children are developing, reinforcing their learning and interacting with others.

Organising staff training

Observation skills need to be fine-tuned. Staff need to ensure that they focus intently on those issues that will give them the most valid information, and are not being distracted by less revealing or important areas. All settings should consider allocating time for staff training in observation techniques and in moderation of their findings. This will be very important if there are staff new to your setting or if you are anxious to include a greater range of staff, and perhaps helpers, in the process.

Useful tip

The 'Observation techniques – individual' photocopiable sheet on page 140 is designed to help you make focused observations, maximise available time and plan the next steps for learning.

> Consult your teacher mentor and determine whether there are appropriate training sessions organised by your LEA and build these into your professional development schedule.

> Send representatives to any LEA sessions and follow this up with your own in-house programme, where those who attended lead the training.

> Consider setting up sessions to be shared with another, or a number of other local settings. This might be very useful for those settings who do not have the advantage of LEA training.

> You might ask your teacher mentor to lead one of your sessions, or ask for a recommendation and obtain the services of another practitioner who can lead training sessions.

> Ask your LEA for any useful support materials, especially video or CD-ROM clips of young children engaged in different activities.

> Obtain a copy of the QCA *Foundation Stage Profile* publication, which includes a CD with examples of children's work, potentially a useful focus for staff discussion and training

> Organise your own independent internal sessions.

Staff training in observation skills

Most settings will have a range of staff experience and all practitioners will have intuitively gleaned information about their children in the normal run of their daily duties. Newly-trained staff entering the profession will have undergone child observation assignments as part of their training courses. Helpers are likely to be parents or adults, who have had good contact with young children. So it will be rare for anyone to be starting absolutely from scratch – and you are likely to find a real reservoir of useful experience to share together!

Most skilled staff will be able to recall many aspects of individual children's development and performance with confidence, particularly from their direct supervision of tasks and activities. However, it is extremely difficult to observe all children intently when you are also running a group session. Generally you are too busy engaging all the children to make tightly-focused, uninterrupted observations. You are usually too involved 'conducting' proceedings without the luxury of enjoying the overall performance!

All settings will need to set up some direct observations, where staff are only involved in observing children, not in supervising the activity. In addition to staff training, children will also need to know that they should not approach staff who are observing activities. Settings will need to think out how this can be best effected. Consider the following models of good practice used for staff training.

Example 1 – a private nursery with a mix of full- and part-time staff

The manager wanted to ensure that all staff felt confident with the observation process and were able to contribute towards their new assessment system. She also wanted to build on the existing good practice, which she knew happened informally, and for part-time staff to feel equally valued as observers. A series of training sessions were planned over the term, held every fortnight for an hour's duration

The programme was as follows:

Session 1

➤ The manager outlined the need for accurate assessment within a manageable system and the importance of being able to pass on firm judgements of their children's progress to the next providers. She stressed that the information that their setting passed on for the first part of the Foundation Stage to school Reception classes was crucial for children's development and the ultimate completion of the *Foundation Stage Profile.*

➤ She went through the setting's current system and ensured that all staff were familiar with it. Staff discussed the ways they gathered information and how this was recorded and shared with parents/carers, giving real examples and sharing the successes or any problems they had encountered.

➤ Staff then discussed the importance of observations in the assessment process. The manager referred to the next week's planning and all staff were asked to select an activity they would be involved in. They were asked to make brief notes about one child who was taking part in the activity, to share at the next meeting.

➤ The manager produced a simple sheet for each member of staff to guide their notes. The headings were:
- who was observed?
- what was the activity?
- was it child-chosen or staff-directed?
- which Areas of Learning were involved?
- what was observed and what learning took place?
- how do you know?

➤ Staff carried out the observations and prepared notes for the next session.

Session 2

➤ The manager recapped on the activity and asked staff to take turns to share their observations, highlighting any difficulties and successes with the process. Other staff were encouraged to ask questions and seek clarifications. The manager constantly helped staff focus on real evidence of learning and how children presented, by asking: 'How do you know?' and, 'What did this behaviour tell you?' and so on.

➤ A flipchart sheet with the headings, 'Observation +' and, 'Observation –' was completed by a member of staff.

➤ After each feedback all staff were asked to suggest ways that the child's learning could be extended. The importance of assessment as a tool for further learning was stressed.

➤ After all feedbacks were completed, staff considered the pluses and minuses and made suggestions to overcome any problems.

➤ Staff were asked to repeat the observation process, following the same child and looking for any progress, before the next training session.

Session 3

➤ Staff gave short feedbacks on their observations as before. The manager encouraged staff to challenge each other gently for evidence!

➤ Staff agreed the elements of successful observation and recorded them. (These were later written up and circulated to be included in all staff folders.)

➤ The manager then introduced a schedule for the next few weeks for a series of ten-minute observations to be carried out (by all staff), where the observer was not involved with the activity.

> Staff were concerned that children would approach them whilst they were observing. They discussed how to introduce the idea to children and agreed they would wear 'SSh! I'm watching quietly' badges, shaped like an eye, which a member of staff offered to make.
> The first staff group carried out the observations before the next session.

Sessions 4 and 5
> Staff openly fed back their observations and thoughts on the success of arrangements. Issues were discussed and adjustments were made to the process. (For example, observations were extended to 15 minutes for outdoor and practical group activities.)
> The manager helped staff draw up a schedule of observations for the following term, focusing on the oldest children, who were due to transfer to other settings, and those other children where evidence was thin or concerns were expressed.

Example 2 – a Reception class with a full-time teacher and nursery nurse
Both staff were keen to ensure that they made accurate judgements and supported each other in assessment. However, they were worried about how they could fit observations into their busy schedule. The teacher had attended LEA training on the *Foundation Stage Profile* requirements, led by teacher mentors, but was concerned that she was the only Reception teacher in her school. Consequently, she wanted wider support.

> She shared with the nursery nurse the information from her training and they discussed how this would affect the organisation.
> They watched the *Foundation Stage Profile* CD examples together and also other video material offered by the LEA. They talked about what they had seen and what evidence there was of children's progress and attainment. They discussed what further information they would need to make secure judgements and what they would expect to see when children had made good progress in the different Areas. They also considered how they would extend the children's learning.
> They made a list of ways they could adapt their practice to build in more observation, and also of their concerns. They agreed that during whole-class sessions led by the teacher, the nursery nurse could observe children by rotation. They also agreed that the nursery nurse could lead certain whole-class activities, or parts of them, whilst the teacher carried out observations of named children.
> They carried out these observations and also swapped 'lead' places during the session, observing the same children and comparing notes afterwards, focusing on what was seen and the evidence this gave for learning.

➤ They designed their own observation sheet, after consulting colleagues at other settings, adapting and personalising the model offered by the LEA.

➤ They made brightly-coloured fabric sashes to wear when they were observing and gradually trained the children to respect this.

➤ They shared the list of concerns with the head teacher and early years coordinator. Some areas were resolved, for example, the head teacher agreed to allocate more occasional but planned classroom support towards the end of the summer term to make observations and assessment easier. Other issues were raised with the teacher mentor and LEA staff, who gave general advice and shared examples of good practice from other settings.

➤ The early years coordinator helped arrange regular sessions with neighbouring schools that had only one Reception class to discuss assessment and moderation issues, with schools taking turns to host meetings.

➤ The early years coordinator also arranged to come into a few lessons and release staff for short observation periods. This also included taking control of the class occasionally, so that the teacher and nursery nurse were able to make short joint observations to moderate their judgements and build confidence.

➤ The head teacher and a parent helper both visited the class and videoed a series of different activities, including outdoor play, home-play and music-making sessions. Staff discussed these together and made agreed joint observations. With parents' and carers' agreement, the videos were used for staff-training sessions with colleague schools.

Involving staff fully

Recognising and using all staff skills, and involving staff to the full, has been a recurrent theme throughout this book. This very much confirms the stance taken in the QCA publications, particularly the *Foundation Stage Profile Handbook*, where the involvement of all staff who have contact with children in any setting's assessment process, is strongly endorsed. All staff can play important roles in the spectrum of planning, assessment and record-keeping – provided this is well managed and everyone is clear about the scope of their roles and how they can make a positive contribution.

Before approaching this section of guidance, it would be useful to read 'Using staff effectively' in Chapter 1, to explore how staff can be involved in the early stages of the process. It would also be helpful to then consider the advice contained in 'The most effective use of staff' in Chapter 4. The main thrust of that section is concerned with the specific roles of designated 'key staff', the work of the SENCO and their interrelationship with other involved staff, dealing with the management issues of establishing a comprehensive overall programme of assessment.

This current chapter builds on the earlier chapters and focuses on ways in which individual staff members can be best involved collecting information that feeds into the assessment of individual children. There is a real danger that assessment comes to dominate a setting's provision, whereas it should just be a normal part of the programme and be strongly rooted in helping practitioners plan the next steps in learning for their charges. Staff need clear guidance on when to make formal assessments, how this will be done and what they are to look for as evidence of attainment and progress. It will be important to give staff some professional training before they embark on a formalised process,

Guiding staff on evidence gathering

The 'Staff roles guide' photocopiable sheet on page 141 will help settings involve a number of different staff members in an effective way. It can be a useful catalyst for staff professional development and should provide a simple agenda to stimulate whole-staff discussions.

Using the 'Staff roles guide' photocopiable sheet for training:

➤ Have your following week's planning to hand.
➤ Identify a child (or children) whose progress and attainment is to be assessed.
➤ Give every member of staff a photocopiable sheet and get them to complete the child's (or children's) name and period of time sections.
➤ Talk about the child (or children) and track which of a range of planned activities they will be directed to or allowed to choose from during the assessment period (session/day/week or other selected timescale).

➤ Ask staff to refer to the planning. Get them to determine which of them will be leading specific activities, or would be able to spend some time observing a planned task, where the child will be engaged.
➤ Ensure that there is good coverage of a sufficient range of different activities. These can be easily spread over several days. When this is agreed, ask staff to add their names to a box and complete the 'In activity' section, stating the exact activity, time and date (if necessary).
➤ Then get all staff to work together to help each colleague in turn. Consider the first activity that will be observed and the children who will be assessed. Discuss what assessment information is already known about each child, for example, if the child has had difficulty relating to others and taking turns, or if they already know some phonics, or how well they can match and sort.
➤ Ask all staff to suggest what progress the child might have made by now. Focus very tightly on what *evidence* there would need to be to indicate this. For example, if the child could now understand that they must wait for their turn and respect the views of others, could the staff member ensure that opportunities to see this will be available? And what would constitute strong evidence of attainment? Stress that one single example would not be enough, although it might indicate positive progress and a growing level of understanding.
➤ Ask staff to consider whether any of their focus activities might also be a source of confirming evidence and, if so, ask them to note it in their box. (If space requires it, more than one box can be used for the same activity.)
➤ Work your way through each member of staff's selected activity and complete the staff boxes.
➤ Finally, agree the feedback time and date and decide how the findings will be shared. If you have part-time staff in your setting, it will be important to devise a system that enables them to share their views. This could be in writing or by reporting to another colleague.
➤ Ensure that another whole-staff training session is scheduled, after all staff have carried out their roles, to discuss how well the process has been working and to pass on all feedback to the child's 'key staff' member. The assessment process can then be further refined and improve as and when it is necessary.

Special educational needs issues

The 'Staff roles guide' photocopiable sheet on page 141 is especially useful for tracking the progress of children with SEN. It enables staff to decide on very specific evidence of progress (or lack of it) and involves the greatest number of staff observing a wide range of different activities. This can provide very powerful and detailed information to share with parents/carers and other support agencies. This will be particularly useful when additional support for a child's special needs (Early Years Action Plus) is being sought from other busy providers.

Involving helpers effectively

Most settings will have volunteer helpers, if not regularly, then occasionally. Many settings by their very nature will encourage – or request – that parents and carers remain with their children for all or some of the time. Some settings arrange a definite and dated rota of helpers, but in others this is a much more casual, day-to-day happening. A few settings will find it very difficult to attract regular helpers, because of parents' work commitments or other local reasons, others will find a large reservoir of interested and available parents/carers. Occasionally settings find that their helpers are reluctant to commit to regular sessions, but are very happy to accompany groups on visits or are willing to respond to direct requests for support at special events, such as Teddy Bears' Tea Parties.

Whatever your setting's circumstances, helpers are a temporary part of your team and are an extra pair of eyes and ears to support your learning programmes and offer information about how well these went. Helpers are often based with children to offer extra adult supervision when staff are intensely engaged in leading other activities. This means they can observe children in activities that other staff may have more limited opportunities to witness. With your guidance such adults can add useful information to your overall assessment procedures.

Security issues

In some settings, especially those attached to schools, helpers may be adults who are not parents/carers of children in the Foundation Stage, or they might be local volunteers. There will be local arrangements that are required for security clearance, and settings must be aware of any regulations that affect them and ensure that all safety-check procedures are followed appropriately. These checks are to ascertain that no adults with direct contact with children have any history which deems them unsuitable in this role, and is obviously necessary to safeguard the welfare of young children. It is a fairly straightforward system to implement, although some parents/carers can be a little anxious, so a sensitive approach is needed. Parents/carers sometimes need reassurance that parking and speeding offences do not render them 'unsuitable' helpers! The confidential checks are carried out by a central clearance organisation after the adult has completed a form and made personal declarations. The whole process can take a few weeks to run its course. If you are in any doubt about how this affects your setting's work with helpers, ask your teacher mentor or local authority and ensure that you have established a process that will cover your circumstances adequately.

There are also sensitive issues to broach with helpers. Their involvement may bring them into contact with their neighbour's children, those with social and behavioural difficulties or with SEN. Settings will need to gently remind helpers

Useful tip
The reverse side of the photocopiable sheet on page 141 could be used for recording comments, or use any of the photocopiable sheets on pages 115-127 to record observations in the six Areas of Learning. These should be passed to the 'key staff' member as appropriate and added to each child's file.

of confidentiality issues and be vigilant that staff do not discuss any 'delicate' issues within earshot. Good practice is to have a 'Helper's brochure' which gives brief details of the daily organisation, personnel and contains key information, including details about safety and security. It should also contains a user-friendly Code of Practice on confidentiality and sensitive issues.

Making the most of parents'/carers' involvement

Parents and carers know their children better than anyone and they are usually a child's first and most enduring educators. Both of the QCA publications, the *Curriculum Guidance for the Foundation Stage* and the *Foundation Stage Profile Handbook,* unequivocally stress the importance of involving parents/carers in their children's learning and in establishing a productive partnership with them from the first contact. There is no doubt that when parents, carers and practitioners work together in early years settings, the results have a very beneficial effect on children's development and learning. Nationally, there is an expectation that parents/carers should be involved in their children's education at all levels, and all settings and schools are required to facilitate this.

It will be helpful to read the guidance 'Parental involvement' in Chapter 5, before working through the next two pages. In Chapter 5, you will find extensive advice on how to develop and refine your parental relationship to include positive approaches to assessment. 'Parental involvement' concentrates on how settings can streamline arrangements to build a programme of parental involvement and understanding of your chosen assessment schedule. It also suggests ways in which parents/carers can contribute to the assessment process. You will find information on how best to tackle initial and ongoing discussions with parents/carers. It also addresses how settings can meet the requirements for parental involvement and recording discussions for the *Foundation Stage Profile,* which Reception classes must have completed by the end of the summer term.

Best practice

It is appropriate to remind all staff of best practice in achieving the most productive partnerships with parents/carers. In the best settings:

➤ practitioners show respect for the role of parents/carers in their child's education
➤ the past and future roles of parents/carers in their children's education are recognised and actively encouraged
➤ practitioners listen carefully to parents/carers' views and their concerns
➤ flexible arrangements are made which enable parents/carers and practitioners to talk together about their children
➤ parents/carers are made to feel welcome and are valued
➤ parents/carers' expertise is sought and used to support learning
➤ practitioners use a variety of ways to inform parents/carers about the curriculum

➤ parents/carers and practitioners work together to share and record information about children
➤ home links and activities are actively encouraged.

Good communications 'health check'

➤ *Do we send out newsletters regularly enough?*
  • how often – too much or not enough?
➤ *How do we rate their quality?*
  • overall appeal?
  • are they personalised to our setting?
  • quality of information?
  • do we share our curriculum?
  • do we include children's work and photos?
  • how do parents rate them? What else would parents like to be included?
  • could parents contribute?
➤ *How good is our brochure?*
  • is it appealing?
  • informative?
  • is anything missing?
  • who gets it?
  • how do parents rate it?
➤ *How positive is our first contact with parents?*
  • is it personal to individual sets of parents?
  • do we have access to all parents?
  • how do we build mutual respect? Can we improve arrangements?
  • do we meet all parents in the same way?
  • how do we jointly establish an entry profile?
➤ *Do we maintain regular individual contact and discuss children's progress?*
  • is it often enough?
  • how is it organised and recorded?
  • what use do we make of the information?
  • how do parents feel about it?
  • do we see all the parents?
  • how do we contact those we don't see?
➤ *What other ways do we keep parents informed?*
  • do we make enough use of noticeboards, videos, photographs or displays?
  • are we providing sufficient information?
  • have we consulted parents for their views?

Good communication

This has to be at the heart of effective parental involvement and most settings work hard to ensure that a flow of useful information is maintained. The time it takes is well spent but needs careful planning. In the hectic atmosphere of a vibrant setting, opportunities to review and improve communications systems are sometimes missed. Try to carry out a 'health check' of your current arrangements on a regular basis, preferably annually, and pinpoint any areas that need adjustment or updating.

Building on home links for assessment

Most settings are keen to build good home links and encourage parents/carers to support their children's further learning at home. It is good practice to send materials and resources home to help parents/carers engage in simple activities with their child. However, settings do not always capitalise on opportunities for parental feedback. With just a little adjustment parents/carers can contribute to the assessment process and see clearly how their children are making progress. The 'Parents' home activity sheets' photocopiable sheets on pages 142 and 143 have been designed to aid this process. The film strip on page 142 is planned in three distinct parts. Settings should complete the first section with the child's name and the idea for a home-extension activity. Busy settings could complete 'Scenes 2 and 3' on one sheet to make the most of time and then photocopy several for distribution home for a whole group of children, letting

parents/carers complete the rest. Alternatively, the sheets could be used on an individual basis, with specific activities for named children, such as those with special educational needs or more able children.

The rocket ship on page 143 has been planned to give a greater focus on how the child views their progress. As before, settings should complete the top 'command module' sections of the rocket, but this time add the 'fin' section naming the person to whom the completed sheet should be sent. Parents/carers, hopefully in consultation with their children, should fill in the remaining sections.

Children can also colour the sheet in if suitable resources are sent home with it, and this could give some indication of fine motor control development. Date them and place in the children's record files once the sheets come back to you.

Both sheets can be used repeatedly with different details added. However, individual settings might like to design their own personalised sheets following a similar pattern.

Working positively with other agencies

Every setting should be aware of the necessity to build productive relationships with a wide range of other agencies that may be encountered as part of your normal work. All settings need to discover details of the specific services operating in their area and draw up a contact list of addresses and named personnel. This information should be available from your local council, education offices and library. The contact list should be displayed in the staff room, so that it is available for immediate use if needed.

The actual nature and range of agencies may vary for different settings, depending on local arrangements and the structure of your local authority services.

These are likely to include:

➤ health services
➤ pre-school support services (through Early Years Partnership Developments)
➤ Social Services
➤ special educational needs services
➤ multicultural support services for support for children with English as Another Language (EAL)
➤ education services (often including library services).

It would be useful for your setting to contact each local service and request details of the support that they offer both to early years settings and to families. By having this knowledge at your fingertips, your setting will be able to access help when you need it most. Often a setting can use this knowledge to help a worried parent make early contact with the right service and gain personal support for their child or difficult family circumstances. You may be able to request a visit from service representatives to talk to you about their services and procedures. However, these agencies are often very pressured and find such sessions difficult to fit into busy schedules. It would maximise their time, and be an excellent partnership activity, if you join together with a group of other local settings and invite a representative to talk to you all. Your teacher mentor or local authority may be able to help you organise this successfully.

Multi-agency files

The welfare and needs of the child should be at the heart of any multi-agency dealings. However, all agencies have their own procedures and constraints, depending on the local organisational structures. A good setting will swiftly familiarise itself with the correct processes for seeking help, obtaining information and referring children for specific support. Delay can result if the established procedures are not followed or correct information is not provided. Make sure that your setting writes out a step-by-step checklist for each agency and has this readily available for staff. Build up a file of available services and keep this up to date. It will also be useful to keep a log of any contacts you make (with reasons and references to any children involved), so that you have all the information together if you need to follow up any outstanding issues. The log should be stored securely because of its confidential nature. This will also give a good record to share with agencies when you are seeking additional support for any children causing you concern, because it easily shows all the avenues you have already explored, and when.

Health services

Be sure to ask all parents/carers at initial meetings for details of any special health issues concerning their child and of any health services that are involved in supporting them. For children with particular medical conditions the local clinic or health services may be able to give you useful advice and resources, but you will need to discuss this with the parents/carers. Good contacts with health services will also mean that you can pass on information to parents/carers or arrange for a nurse or health worker to give short talks to your parents/carers on topical health issues and answer any questions.

Social Services

Some of your families may be in contact with social workers. Although this is a sensitive area, try to ascertain whether it is the case by asking parents/carers if they are working with any support services – but remember that some families may be reluctant to share this information with you. Be warm and open and offer to help in any way you can, including meeting any allocated social worker and offering your setting at a quiet time for family meetings.

Remember that every setting needs to have a Child Protection Policy. (School settings will adhere to the overall school policy.) This policy needs to include information about what constitutes 'child protection' issues, what to look for and what procedures must be followed in the event of any concerns. It should be clear on how any referral must be made and how parents/carers have to be involved – often a difficult area for staff. Referrals are normally made to the Social Services Department and you can turn to them for advice on how to discuss any concerns with parents/carers. In the case of suspected sexual abuse, staff *must* speak to Social Services before approaching parents/carers.

Special needs support services

You need to familiarise yourself with the precise local arrangements for seeking support, as these can vary from area to area. However, all settings are expected to admit and support children with SEN, adjusting their programmes to give specific support for children who need Early Years Action. Your setting can seek advice from special needs support services on how to help any identified children. These services can sometimes loan specialist equipment and resources. Where children fail to make the progress they should even with additional support, you need to know the local procedures for referring children to secure Early Years Action Plus support. In most cases you will need to provide detailed evidence of the support you have provided and the results of this.

The 'SEN observation record' photocopiable sheet on page 144 been designed with this in mind. This form can be used as a prompt for relating activities and support to any child's IEP. It is also an observation agenda to ensure vital evidence is gathered and is clear. It can then be shared with SEN services when there is a need for referrals and review. The sheets can be used repeatedly over time to give a detailed picture of any child's responses, difficulties and needs, which will help your setting present in any case requesting additional specialist support.

Audit your provision for **Personal, social and emotional development**

Note examples in your setting

Requirements	Daily pattern/ organisation	Environment	Adult roles	Resources	Themes and topics	Play areas
Children can: - learn respect for self and others - value own/other cultures - develop social skills - build positive relationships - learn sensitivity - develop positive attitudes to learning - make choices, solve problems.						
Practitioners: - offer positive role models - build on children's interests - plan challenging activities - extend children's vocabulary - encourage good manners and social skills - use open-ended questions - provide a stimulating environment (inside and outside) - encourage independence.						

Areas for further development:

Audit your provision for Communication, language and literacy

Note examples in your setting

Requirements	Daily pattern/ organisation	Environment	Adult roles	Resources	Themes and topics	Play areas
Children can: - listen to others - speak about ideas and events - use language constantly - develop joy in books, rhymes, poems - delight in sounds and words - work in a literacy rich environment.						
Practitioners: - encourage all forms of communication - develop children's confidence - provide motivating activities - offer stimulating areas - stress listening, taking turns to speak, question and share ideas - model new vocabulary - model different language use - encourage thinking aloud - surround children with language activities.						

Areas for further development:

Audit your provision for **Mathematical development**

Note examples in your setting

Requirements	Daily pattern/ organisation	Environment	Adult roles	Resources	Themes and topics	Play areas
Children can: - play/experiment with mathematical resources - engage in mathematical role-play - play mathematical games - talk about mathematical activities.						
Practitioners: - promote positive attitude to mathematics - extend mathematics in a wide range of activities - encourage different ways to record - plan a balanced programme (number, shape and measures, making connections, relationships) - use mathematical language - use mathematical questions - encourage mathematical talk - create a numerate environment - encourage children to become confident mathematicians.						

Areas for further development:

Audit your provision for **Knowledge and understanding of the world**

Note examples in your setting

Requirements	Daily pattern/ organisation	Environment	Adult roles	Resources	Themes and topics	Play areas
Children can: - experience a balance of all aspects of this area - engage in practical activities - experiment with different tools, materials and resources - explore the environment - handle current/past artefacts - learn specific skills - interact with adults/visitors - gather information from materials, visits and artefacts.						
Practitioners: - model inquiry approaches - use correct technical vocabulary - teach skills and knowledge - interact and use open-ended questions - make use of the environment - provide exciting resources - involve parents and visitors - organise visits.						

Areas for further development:

Audit your provision for **Physical development**

Note examples in your setting

Requirements	Daily pattern/ organisation	Environment	Adult roles	Resources	Themes and topics	Play areas
Children can: - learn from mistakes and improve movements - take part in frequent physical activity - learn control of large and small scale movements - engage in regular outdoor physical activities - learn through all senses - practise skills - work independently.						
Practitioners: - plan frequent indoor/outdoor physical activities - create safe spaces - encourage appropriate clothing - use action rhymes and songs - plan use of wide range of tools, equipment and resources - use movement vocabulary - directly teach safe techniques - ensure all have access to a range of physical activities.						

Areas for further development:

Audit your provision for Creative development

Note examples in your setting

Requirements	Daily pattern/ organisation	Environment	Adult roles	Resources	Themes and topics	Play areas
Children can: - enjoy a rich exciting learning environment - have their work valued - explore and experiment - enjoy music art, craft, dance, imaginative role-play - test out ideas and talk about them - express themselves with all their senses - use a wide variety of materials, art, music and dance.						
Practitioners: - let children develop own ideal - give time for experimentation - create an alluring environment - plan a wide range of creative activities - provide good resources - plan for artistic visits/visitors - use correct creative vocabulary.						

Areas for further development:

Planning, assessing and record keeping early years training & management

What makes our setting unique?

Review your setting's situation and consider any adjustments/emphasis you should make to your curriculum.

Features of our setting	Implications for our curriculum
Characteristics of our area? (Settled/mobile/high unemployment)	
Family employment patterns?	
Family structures? (Dual/sole parents; large/small/extended)	
Cultural diversity (Main cultures and religions)	
Children with English as an additional language? (English spoken at home/early stage/secure)	
Social backgrounds?	
Accommodation types? (Flats – no gardens; houses – large/small gardens and play areas; estates; traditional; Housing Association; hostels and temporary etc.)	
Children with special educational needs?	
Differences in year groups?	
Attainment on entry? - strengths - weaknesses	
Gender balance?	
Other unique factors?	

Maximising our unique local resources

Review the features available in your locality

Library	Park	Post Office	Market	Supermarket	Local shops	Garage	Others:-
Swimming pool	Leisure centre	Factories	Art gallery	Church	Temples	Mosques	Others:-
Garden centre	Hotels	Doctors	Dentist	Vet	Clinic	Hospital	Others:-
Ambulance	Fire station	Train station	Bus station	Schools	Colleges	Cinemas	Others:-

We already use/visit/link with:	Theme/topic/learning area/link

We could develop links with:	To extend theme/topic/learning area...

PHOTOCOPIABLE

Planning, assessing and record keeping

early years
training & management

Long-term planning grid

(Enlarge two copies to cover one year)

Month:	Themes and topics	Special events and activities	Areas of Learning	Specific aspects	Specific aspects	Specific aspects	Specific aspects	Specific aspects	Specific aspects
			PSED						
			CLL						
			MD						
			KUW						
			PD						
			CD						

Medium-term planning grid

(Photocopy four grids for each term)

Themes and topics:-

Term:

Week No:-	Areas of Learning – Key activities and events						
	PSED	CLL	MD	KUW	PD	CD	

SCHOLASTIC

Planning, assessing and record keeping   early years training & management

Short-term planning grid

(Photocopy four grids for each term)

Week beginning:	MONDAY	Key adult	TUESDAY	Key adult	WEDNESDAY	Key adult	THURSDAY	Key adult	FRIDAY	Key adult
-Themed links/ special events										
PSED activity										
Reading/writing										
New vocabulary										
Maths										
Investigation										
Science										
ICT										
Sand/water play										
Physical - indoor - outdoor										
Creative activities										
Imaginative play										
Role-play										

PHOTOCOPIABLE

Learning objectives assessment form

Theme/topic:-			Date:	Length of observation:
Activity		Target children:		

Area of Learning   **PSED**   **CLL**   **MD**   **KUW**   **PD**   **CD**   (Ring as appropriate)

Stepping Stone:

ELG:

Precise learning objective – what we want children to learn

Children's responses – evidence of what they know, understand and can do
List significant comments, actions, behaviour, attitude of each child observed.

1. Child's name _____

What does this tell us?

2. Child's name _____

What does this tell us?

Our assessment cycle planner

1. Gathering previous information

When do we do it?

How do we do it?

Who does it?

What happens to the information?

2. First parent/carer contact

What do we want to know?

How will we get the information?

Who does it?

What happens to the information?

3. First admission

How are children admitted?

When?

How are parents/carers involved?

What do we want to know?

What happens to the information?

Discuss the issues and fill in the agreed answers to the cycle questions.

4. After settling in

When do we observe?

Who does it?

How do we compare this with previous information?

How are parents/carers involved?

What happens to our information?

5. Regular, timed progress checks

When?

How often?

Who does it?

How is it recorded?

How are parents/carers involved?

6. How do we summarise progress and attainment?

How do we summarise progress and attainment?

Who does it?

When?

What records do we use?

How are these shared with parents/carers?

Who are they passed on to?

Nursery 'Value Added' sheet

(Complete the sections on entry, and compare with the completed leaving page)

Date of entry:- _____ (cohort year)

On entry:-

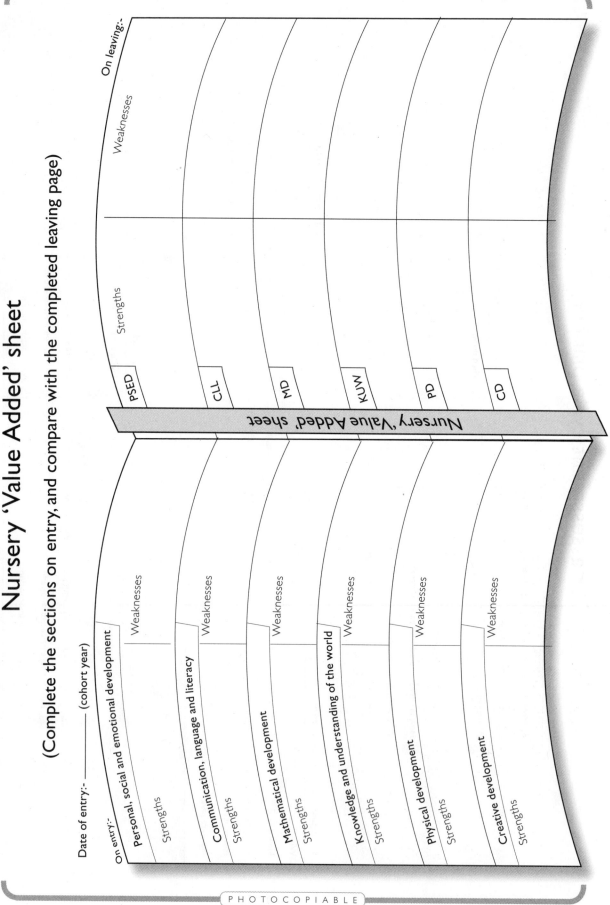

On leaving:-

Weaknesses

Strengths

PSED

CLL

MD

KUW

PD

CD

Nursery 'Value Added' sheet

Personal, social and emotional development — Weaknesses / Strengths

Communication, language and literacy — Weaknesses / Strengths

Mathematical development — Weaknesses / Strengths

Knowledge and understanding of the world — Weaknesses / Strengths

Physical development — Weaknesses / Strengths

Creative development — Weaknesses / Strengths

Planning, assessing and record keeping

early years
**training &
management**

Reception – literacy and numeracy timeline planner

(Decide which literacy/numeracy aspects will be covered and when, then complete the grid)

Autumn term		Spring term		Summer term		Half-term
Literacy aspects	Numeracy aspects	Literacy aspects	Numeracy aspects	Literacy aspects/sessions	Numeracy aspects/sessions	
				Full literacy sessions will be in place by:-	Full numeracy sessions will be in place by:-	

OFSTED inspection checklist

Our Provision	Yes/No	How do we know? What can we show inspectors?
We plan to the *Curriculum Guidance for the Foundation Stage* and our curriculum is based on this.		
We cover all six Areas of Learning fully.		
There is a proper balance of all six Areas of Learning over time. We plan to use Stepping Stones and ELGs.		
Our activities are lively and imaginative.		
We have both directed, and child-initiated activities and play.		
Adults interact well with children to extend their learning.		
Children of different ages and abilities are properly supported and challenged.		
Children with SEN are supported.		
Children with EAL are supported.		
Staff are actively deployed to help targeted groups/individuals.		
Staff assess on a day-to-day basis and adjust their teaching.		
Helpers know how to support the children they work with.		
We have an effective induction programme.		
Parents/carers are involved in discussions about their children.		
Parents/carers are encouraged to be involved in their child's education.		
We have a manageable assessment and recording system.		

Planning, assessing and record keeping

System review

Use the checklist to review your assessment systems and identify any areas that need further development

How are we doing?	Not enough	Enough	Very well	We need to:
Our system reflects the Stepping Stones and ELGs in all six Areas of Learning				
We keep careful assessments of each child				
We have pre-entry information from: parents/carers - other settings - other agencies -				
We make early observations and assessments to plan future work for: individuals - groups -				
We share information with parents/carers: early on - termly - regularly -				
We target children and make regular observation sheets				
We have clear individual records				
We use: samples of work - photographs - notes -				
We pass on clear information to other settings				

Early days assessment

A focus for observations and assessment of initial entry for your setting and to share with parents

Setting

Child's name _____   Date of entry _____

Pre-entry visits: (dates)	Home visits:
Activities undertaken:	Any significant issues:
Any significant issues:	

Observations (after two weeks settling in)

Activity and area (PSED/CLL/MD/KUW/PD/CD)	Interaction with adults/ children	Observation notes

Issues for future learning:

Home support ideas:

Six Areas of Learning – assessment focus sheet 1

Personal, social and emotional development   Child's name _____

Disposition and attitudes

Elements	Observations			Date of achievement
	1	2	3	
1. Shows an interest in classroom activities through observation or participation.				
2. Dresses, undresses and manages own personal hygiene with adult support.				
3. Displays high levels of involvement in self-chosen activities.				
4. Dresses and undresses independently and manages own personal hygiene.				
5. Selects and uses activities and resources independently.				
6. Continues to be interested, motivated and excited to learn.				
7. Is confident to try new activities, initiate ideas. Speaks out in a familiar group.				
8. Maintains attention and concentrates.				
9. Sustains involvement and perseveres, particularly when trying to solve a problem to reach a satisfactory conclusion				

Date	Observation notes and evidence	Element	Next steps ...

PHOTOCOPIABLE

Six Areas of Learning – assessment focus sheet 2

Personal, social and emotional development   Child's name _____

Social development

Elements	Observations			Date of achievement
	1	2	3	
1. Plays alongside others.				
2. Builds relationships through gesture and talk.				
3. Takes turns and shares with adult support.				
4. Works as part of a group or class, taking turns and sharing fairly.				
5. Forms good relationships with adults and peers.				
6. Understands that there need to be agreed values and codes of behaviour for groups of people, including adults and children, to work together harmoniously.				
7. Understands that people have different needs, views, cultures and beliefs that need to be treated with respect.				
8. Understands that s/he can expect others to treat her or his needs, views, cultures and beliefs with respect.				
9. Sustains involvement and perseveres, particularly when trying to solve a problem to reach a satisfactory conclusion.				

Date	Observation notes and evidence	Element	Next steps ....

PHOTOCOPIABLE

◾SCHOLASTIC

early years
training & management

Six Areas of Learning – assessment focus sheet 3

Personal, social and emotional development   Child's name _____

Emotional development

Elements	Observations			Date of achievement
	1	2	3	
1. Separates from main carer with support.				
2. Communicates freely about home and community.				
3. Expresses needs and feelings in appropriate ways.				
4. Responds to significant experiences, showing a range of feelings when appropriate.				
5. Has a developing awareness of own needs, views and feelings and is sensitive to the needs, views and feelings of others.				
6. Is developing respect for own culture and beliefs and those of other people.				
7. Considers the consequences of words and actions for self and others.				
8. Understands what is right and what is wrong.				
9. Displays a strong sense of self-identity and is able to express and range of emotions fluently and appropriately.				

Date	Observation notes and evidence	Element	Next steps ...

Six Areas of Learning – assessment focus sheet 4

Communication, language and literacy   Child's name _____

Language for communication and thinking

Elements	Observations			Date of achievement
	1	2	3	
1. Listens and responds.				
2. Initiates communication with others, displaying greater confidence in more informal contexts.				
3. Talks activities through, reflecting on and modifying actions.				
4. Listens with enjoyment to stories, songs, rhymes and poems, sustains attentive listening and responds with relevant comments, questions or actions.				
5. Uses language to imagine and recreate roles and experiences.				
6. Interacts with others in a variety of contexts, negotiating plans and activities and taking turns in conversation.				
7. Uses talk to organise, sequence and clarify thinking, ideas, feelings and events, exploring the meanings of sounds of new words.				
8. Speaks clearly with confidence and control, showing awareness of the listener.				
9. Talks and listens confidently and with control, consistently showing awareness of the listener by including relevant detail. Uses language to work out and clarify ideas, showing control of a range of appropriate vocabulary.				

Date	Observation notes and evidence	Element	Next steps ...

Six Areas of Learning – assessment focus sheet 5

Communication, language and literacy   Child's name _____

Linking sounds and letters

Elements	Observations			Date of achievement
	1	2	3	
1. Joins in with rhyming and rhythmic activities.				
2. Shows an awareness of rhyme and alliteration.				
3. Links some sounds to letters.				
4. Links sounds to letters, naming and sounding letters of the alphabet.				
5. Hears and says initial and final sounds in words.				
6. Hears and says short vowel sounds within words.				
7. Use phonics knowledge to read simple regular words.				
8. Attempts to read more complex words, using phonic knowledge.				
9. Uses knowledge of letters, sounds and words when reading and writing independently.				

Date	Observation notes and evidence	Element	Next steps ...

Six Areas of Learning – assessment focus sheet 6

Communication, language and literacy   Child's name _____

Writing

Elements	Observations			Date of achievement
	1	2	3	
1. Experiments with mark-making, sometimes ascribing meaning to the marks.				
2. Uses some clearly identifiable letters to communicate meaning.				
3. Represents some sounds correctly in writing.				
4. Writes own name and other names from memory.				
5. Holds a pencil and uses it effectively to form recognisable letters, most of which are correctly formed.				
6. Attempts writing for a variety of purposes, using features of different forms.				
7. Uses phonics knowledge to write simple regular words and make phonetically plausible attempts at complete words.				
8. Begins to form captions and simple sentences, sometimes using punctuation.				
9. Communicates meaning through phrases and simple sentences with some consistency in punctuation.				

Date	Observation notes and evidence	Element	Next steps ...

PHOTOCOPIABLE

Six Areas of Learning – assessment focus sheet 7

Communication, language and literacy   Child's name _____

Reading

Elements	Observations			Date of achievement
	1	2	3	
1. Is developing an interest in books.				
2. Knows that print conveys meaning.				
3. Recognises a few familiar words.				
4. Knows that in English, print is read from left to right and from top to bottom.				
5. Shows an understanding of the elements of stories, such as main character, sequence of events and openings.				
6. Reads a range of familiar and common words and simple sentences independently.				
7. Retells narratives in the correct sequence, drawing on language patterns of stories.				
8. Shows an understanding of how information can be found in non-fiction texts to answer questions about where, who, why and how.				
9. Reads books of own choice with some fluency and accuracy.				

Date	Observation notes and evidence	Element	Next steps ...

PHOTOCOPIABLE

Six Areas of Learning – assessment focus sheet 8

Mathematical development   Child's name _____

Numbers as labels and for counting

Elements	Observations			Date of achievement
	1	2	3	
1. Says some number names in familiar contexts, such as number rhymes.				
2. Counts reliably up to 3 everyday objects.				
3. Counts reliably up to 6 everyday objects.				
4. Says number names in order.				
5. Recognise numerals 1 to 9.				
6. Counts reliably up to 10 everyday objects.				
7. Orders numbers up to 10.				
8. Uses developing mathematical ideas and methods to solve practical problems.				
9. Recognises, counts, orders and writes numerals up to 20.				

Date	Observation notes and evidence	Element	Next steps ...

PHOTOCOPIABLE

 SCHOLASTIC

Planning, assessing and record keeping

 early years training & management

Six Areas of Learning – assessment focus sheet 9

Mathematical development   Child's name _____

Calculating

Elements	Observations			Date of achievement
	1	2	3	
1. Responds to the vocabulary involved in addition and subtraction in rhymes and games.				
2. Recognises differences in quantity when comparing sets of objects.				
3. Finds one more and one less when comparing objects from a group of up to 5 objects.				
4. Relates addition to combining two groups.				
5. Relates subtraction to taking away.				
6. In practical activities and discussion, begins to use the vocabulary involved in adding and subtracting.				
7. Finds one more or one less than a number from 1–10.				
8. Uses developing mathematical ideas and methods to solve practical problems.				
9. Uses a range of strategies for addition and subtraction, including some mental recall of number bonds.				

Date	Observation notes and evidence	Element	Next steps ...

Six Areas of Learning – assessment focus sheet 10

Mathematical development   Child's name _____

Shape, space and measures

Elements	Observations			Date of achievement
	1	2	3	
1. Experiments with a range of objects and materials showing some mathematical awareness.				
2. Sorts or matches objects and talks about sorting.				
3. Describes shape in simple models, pictures and patterns.				
4. Talks about, recognises and recreates simple patterns.				
5. Uses everyday words to describe position.				
6. Uses languages such as 'circle' or 'bigger' to describe the shape and size of solids and flat shapes.				
7. Uses language such as 'greater', 'smaller', 'heavier' or 'lighter' to compare quantities.				
8. Uses developing mathematical ideas and methods to solve practical problems.				
9. Uses mathematical language to describe solid (3-D) objects and flat (2-D) shapes.				

Date	Observation notes and evidence	Element	Next steps ...

Planning, assessing and record keeping   early years training & management

Six Areas of Learning – assessment focus sheet 11

Knowledge and understanding of the world   Child's name _____

Elements	Observations			Date of achievement
	1	2	3	
1. Shows curiosity and interest by exploring surroundings.				
2. Observes, selects and manipulates objects and materials. Identifies simple features and significant personal events.				
3. Identifies obvious similarities and differences when exploring and observing. Constructs in a purposeful way, using simple tools and techniques.				
4. Investigates places, objects, materials and living things, by using all the senses as appropriate. Identifies some features and talks about those features s/he likes and dislikes.				
5. Ask questions about why things happen and how things work. Looks closely at similarities, differences, patterns and change.				
6. Finds out about past and present events in his/her own life and in those of family members and other people s/he knows. Begins to know about own culture and beliefs and those of other people.				
7. Finds out about and identifies the uses of everyday technology and uses information and communication technology and programmable toys to support her/his work where necessary.				
8. Builds and constructs with a wide range of objects, selecting appropriate resources, tools and techniques and adapting her/ his work where necessary.				
9. Communicates simple planning for investigations and construction and makes simple records and evaluations of her/his work. Identifies and names key features and properties, sometimes linking different experiences, observations and events. Begins to explore what it means to belong to a variety of groups and communities.				

Date	Observation notes and evidence	Element	Next steps ...

Six Areas of Learning – assessment focus sheet 12

Physical development   Child's name _____

Elements	Observations			Date of achievement
	1	2	3	
1. Moves spontaneously, showing some control and coordination.				
2. Moves with confidence in a variety of ways, showing some awareness of space.				
3. Usually shows appropriate control in large and small-scale movements.				
4. Moves with confidence, imagination and in safety. Travels around, under, over and through balancing and climbing equipment. Shows awareness of space, of self and of others.				
5. Demonstrates fine motor control and coordination.				
6. Uses small and large equipment, showing a range of basic skills.				
7. Handles tools, objects, construction and malleable materials safely and with basic control.				
8. Recognises the importance of keeping healthy and those things which contribute to this. Recognises the changes that happen to her/his body when she/he is active.				
9. Repeats, links and adapts simple movements, sometimes commenting on her/his work. Demonstrates coordination and control in large and small movements and using a wide range of tools and equipment.				

Date	Observation notes and evidence	Element	Next steps ...

PHOTOCOPIABLE

Planning, assessing and record keeping

Six Areas of Learning – assessment focus sheet 13

Creative development   Child's name _____

Elements	Observations			Date of achievement
	1	2	3	
1. Explores different media and responds to a variety of sensory experiences. Engages in representational play.				
2. Creates simple representations of events, people and objects and engages in music making.				
3. Tries to capture experiences using a variety of different media.				
4. Sings simple songs from memory.				
5. Explores colour, texture, shape, form and space in 2 or 3 dimensions.				
6. Recognises and explores how sound can be changed. Recognises repeated sounds and sound patterns and matches movements to music.				
7. Uses imagination in art and design, music, dance, imaginative and role play and stories. Responds in a variety of ways to what s/he sees, hears, smell, touches and feels.				
8. Expresses and communicates ideas, thoughts and feelings using a range of materials, suitable tools, imaginative and role play, movement, designing and making, and a variety of songs and musical instruments.				
9. Expresses feelings and preferences in response to artwork, drama, and music and makes some comparisons and links between different pieces. Responds to own work and that of others when exploring and communicating ideas, feelings and preferences through art, music, dance role-play and imaginative play.				

Date	Observation notes and evidence	Element	Next steps ...

Planning for learning

To be completed after observations, to be shared with colleagues and used for planning future activities

Child's name _____

Key points from observation

What the child does well:-

Areas that need more support:-

How can we build this into our programme?

(Activities, staff support, directed tasks, directed groups, home links)

What?	Who?	When?

Planning, assessing and record keeping

early years
training & management

Target group

To be completed after observations, to be shared with colleagues and used for planning future activities

Group activity	Special focus	Learning objective (What is to be learned)	Date:
			Time:

(1) Child's name _____
Significant responses

(2) Child's name _____
Significant responses

(3) Child's name _____
Significant responses

(4) Child's name _____
Significant responses

(5) Child's name _____
Significant responses

(6) Child's name _____
Significant responses

Issues for further learning:

Undirected-play observation

Complete a record in columns 1 and 2, then reflect and complete column 3

General activity:-   Date: Time:

Participating children (* star those targeted)	What happened (content, participation, choices, perseverance, cooperation, collaboration, problem-solving, communication, use of knowledge, skills, individual's contribution)	Related Areas of Learning (to be completed later)
Observer:	**Overall summary comments and issues to follow up**	

early years
training & management

Outdoor-play observation

Focus on one child and record observations in as many areas as possible

PSED

Note significant observations/examples

Note significant comments for CLL

CD

PD

Range of activities – list all and ring those child chooses

Child's name:

Date:

CLL

MD

Note significant observations/examples

Note significant evidence for MD

KUW

Home role-play observation

Note evidence/quotes to support learning

Activity: _____

Child's name: _____

Date: _____

Add photograph of activity here

This photograph shows...

Evidence of learning/child's contribution to role-play

PSED	CLL
MD	KUW
PD	CD

Child's assessment

Enlarge and laminate to make activity learning objective cards

We are learning...

We are practising...

We are...

Individual record title page

Personalise the template for your setting's use

Attach a photo of the child taken during his/her first days at school.

Child's name _____

Date of birth _____   Entry date _____

Class / Group _____   Date _____

_____   _____

_____   _____

Parents' entry contribution

A model for initial discussions with new parents or carers to add to each child's records

Child's name _____ Date of birth _____

Position in family _____

Name of parents or guardian _____

Any access arrangements _____

_____

Who will bring the child to the setting? _____

Special medical conditions (asthma, allergies) _____

_____

Any physical conditions/considerations (glasses, hearing)

_____

Special interests, likes and skills _____

_____

Dislikes _____

_____

Special friends _____

_____

Favourite toys/games _____

Pets _____

Any other issues _____

PHOTOCOPIABLE

Parents' ongoing contribution

An agenda for discussions with parents/carers throughout your setting.

Child's name _____ Date of birth _____

Present _____

Attendance/absences? _____

Comments _____

Behaviour/confidence? _____

Comments _____

Progress since entry/task discussions and new targets

Personal, social and emotional development	Communication, language and literacy	Mathematical development
New targets:-		
Knowledge and understanding of the world	Physical development	Creative development
New targets:-		

Parents'/carers' views

Practitioner _____ Parent/carer _____

Child's record sheet – early days

Complete alongside the child after a few weeks in your setting

Child's name _____

Date _____

I like to

I am good at

I don't like to

I find it hard to

My special friends are

I like them because

At home I like

Child's record sheet – ongoing

Complete regularly alongside children well-established in your setting

Child's name _____

Date _____

My favourite things are

I am good at

I am getting better at

I don't like to

I am working hard at

My best friends are

I would like to

Passing on information

A model for summary information to be given to other settings

Our setting

Address and contact

Child's name _____ Date of birth _____

Date of entry _____ Date of leaving _____

Attendance _____ Health issues _____

Favourite activities _____

_____

Special friends _____

Special medical conditions (asthma, allergies etc.) _____

Summary of attainments

Personal, social and emotional development	Communication, language and literacy	Mathematical development
Knowledge and understanding of the world	Physical development	Creative development

Other records are attached for

Other comments:-

Signed _____ Role _____ Date _____

Observation techniques – individual

Prepare the sheet ahead of the observation and then use as a focus

Observed activity

Main Area of Learning – (Stepping Stone/ELG)

Personal targets (IEP, SEN, EAL)

More practice needed on

Name
Date
Length of observation
Observer

Contribution of other Areas of Learning

What the child did and said

What the child learned

How I know

Planning, assessing and record keeping

early years
training &
management

Staff roles guide

Complete and discuss with staff so that all are clear of what their contribution should be

Today/this session/this week/ _____ we are assessing _____ 's progress. This is how the team can help gather secure evidence of development.

Staff name _____
Please look for evidence of:

In activity

Staff name _____
Please look for evidence of:

In activity

Staff name _____
Please look for evidence of:

In activity

Staff name _____
Please look for evidence of:

In activity

Thank you!

Be ready to share your thoughts

on _____ at _____

with _____

_____

Parents' home activity sheet 1

Complete and send home to parents

We are delighted that you are going to do some activities at home. We hope this guide will help you and we would like to know how it goes!

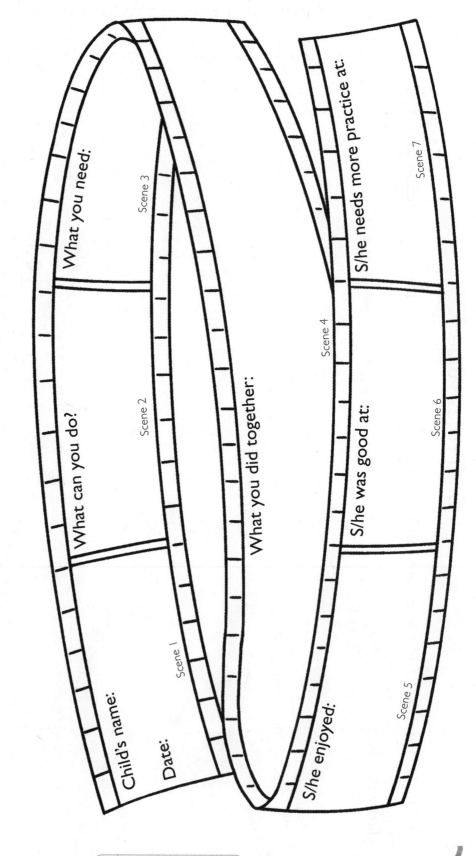

Child's name:

Date:

Scene 1

What can you do?

Scene 2

What you need:

Scene 3

What you did together:

Scene 4

S/he enjoyed:

Scene 5

S/he was good at:

Scene 6

S/he needs more practice at:

Scene 7

Parents' home activity sheet 2

Complete the top two segments and share with parents

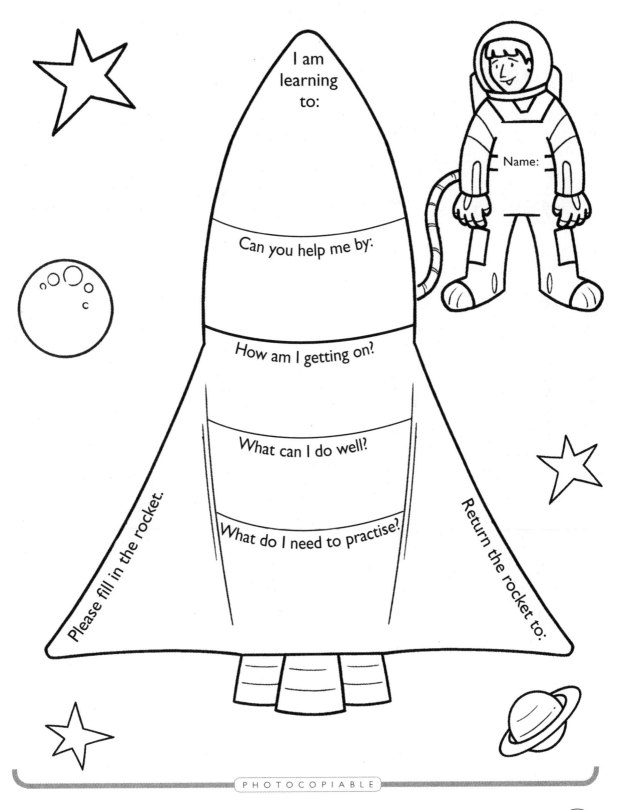

I am learning to:

Can you help me by:

How am I getting on?

What can I do well?

What do I need to practise?

Name:

Please fill in the rocket.

Return the rocket to:

SEN observation record

Complete the observation sheet for individual children with SEN

Child's name _____ Age _____ Date of birth _____

Nature of SEN

	How was this reflected in the activity?
Early Years Action What does the IEP say? Targets? Additional provision? Teaching approaches? Review date?	

Activity undertaken

How did the child present?

Attitude/behaviour?

Interaction with others?

What did the child do well?

What did the child find difficult?

What support is needed for further learning?